VOICES
in the
WIND

By

BOYD RICHARDSON

To Darla L. (Hanks) Isackson and Tory C. Anderson, my two editors, along with my wife, Margie and my six sons who make up my writing team. "No man is an island," the poet said, and it's true. There are few things in this world we can do alone.

Printed in the United States of America
Library of Congress Catalog Card Number 92–071089
Covenant Communications, Inc.
Voices in the Wind
First Printing July 1992
Cover Art by Wayne Andreason
Cover Design by Leslie X. Goodman
ISBN 1–55503–393–8

ABOUT THE AUTHOR

Boyd Richardson first became interested in the past when he transcribed several volumes of oral histories. When his sons complained that they had read all the LDS fiction in the county library, Boyd used the knowledge he gained from working with those oral histories and started writing short stories. *Voices in the Wind* was originally one of those stories. His writing begins in his head while he rides the bus or jogs with a son. (Boyd jogs forty miles a week).

Boyd graduated from Brigham Young University and filled a proselyting mission to the East Central states. Less than a year after he returned home he accepted a Labor Mission call, thus serving four-and-a-half years as a full-time missionary.

Shortly after returning from his labor mission, he met and married Margie Powell of Lehi. They have five "homemade" sons and one "imported"—an adopted Korean son. With so many boys in the family Boyd and Margie have become deeply involved with Scouting (both are Silver Beaver Scouters). Five of their six sons are Eagle Scouts, and the sixth soon will be. Their two oldest sons are returned missionaries; their third son is now on a mission in Norway.

Boyd is employed as a security officer at the Church Office Building in Salt Lake City. He says, "I'm just your basic line security officer that directs traffic, stands posts, and walks beats in all kinds of weather. In short, I'm a working man, and my writings show it. I take joy in memorizing scriptures as I walk my beat. However, there's no danger of me becoming a scriptorian because I too often forget the scriptures I memorize! Still, my stories are laced with scriptural themes although my readers may not initially notice. Charity—the pure love of Christ—is my favorite theme."

Boyd enjoys the education process and has continued to take classes since his graduation from college. He has always been active in the Church and in the Scouting program. He is currently the White Buffalo district Boy Scout vice chairman in the West Jordan Stake.

• Chapter One •

Mae

They were five rough men, the scum of the earth. Well mounted, they set their horses blocking our path. We were in trouble, two women and a boy, alone. The wide expanse of the Texas panhandle spread before us with its big, blue sky. But maybe we were no longer in Texas, maybe we were in eastern Colorado . . . who knows?

I'm Mae, Mae Brisk. Mama's name is Julienne, and my little brother who's seven, is Hector. He didn't understand what was going on. Course I'm not sure any of us understood.

We were expecting Indians, but what we got was white trash. They came down from the Indian Nation, I suppose. Two were dressed in buckskins, and the other three were wearing rags that sorely needed to see the inside of a wash tub.

Well, they just set their horses and looked at us, just a-grinning like they'd done something high and mighty. I was just a skinny fifteen-year-old girl who had never been anywhere and didn't know much about the ways of the world. But I'd heard tell there were men out there, in the big wide world, who were almighty bad, and these men must be some of them.

"You just step down, ma'am, and we'll have a look at your wagon," one rider announced.

"We've nothing of interest to you," Mama replied.

"You've got food, and we haven't had a decent woman-cooked meal in weeks. So you just get down, start a fire, and get a'cookin'."

"Winter squash and corn meal, that's all we have," Mama responded. It was all we'd had for days, though we had a lot of it. The rider threw Mama a hard look that told her she better get moving. So Mama climbed down from the wagon and started a fire and stirred up a pot of corn meal mush. It didn't take her long, and when it was ready they sat right down and wolfed it down like they'd not eaten such fine vittles in all their born days.

While Mama was cooking the mush, they were going through our wagon like a cyclone, leaving nothing untouched. "You've got nothing of value," one man complained, "'cept the mules, so we'll take 'em."

"If'n you take the mules," Mama said, quietly, looking into the eyes of the spokesman, "we're as good as dead."

"Yes, ma'am, you surely are. But one old woman, alone, out here with two little dirty rat-tails, won't last long nohow."

Being called a dirty rat-tail made me mad. Oh, it did make me mad! I looked down at my dress. I'd worn it on the trail all week, and it looked as much. I wanted to cry, but held my tears, 'cause I didn't want to act like a rat-tail kid.

"You'll hang as a horse thief!" Mama said. Course she knew as well as I did that they wouldn't—'cause they wouldn't get caught.

One rider grinned. "Who'll hang us?"

We could do nothing as they rounded up our stock, including the milk cows and the buckskin colt, and drove away with 'em.

If we hadn't been alone, we wouldn't have made such easy prey. We didn't start out alone; we started out ten wagons strong, but some turned back. Then the disease struck.

Smallpox. It struck hard, and when it killed, the dead were sorely missed.

It was 1864, and in the East our menfolks were bleeding for the 'cause of the Confederacy, which had claimed Papa's life. He was killed at Shiloh, they say. The war left Texas almighty bare of decent menfolks, but there were shysters aplenty.

Running north and south through Texas is the Cross Timbers, a forest of post oak and scrub oak, called blackjack. Mixed in are patches of prickly pear. But near the streams are patches of beautiful dogwood, redbud, and persimmon. It's a hard land to travel across, but a great land for collecting wild honey.

On the east side was our farm and a good one too. But we had a mortgage, and with a lack of menfolks to work the fields, the mortgage couldn't be met. Papa wouldn't have put us in that kind of a bind a'purpose, but he thought he'd be gone only a few months, a year at the most. When Papa left, the mortgage was owned by Mr. McPhee. After Papa died, Mr. McPhee sold the mortgage to shysters and sold us out in the process.

"There's gold in Oregon," it was said. "You can either hunt gold yourself, or raise crops to sell to those who do hunt gold." So, with nothing to lose, we joined eleven other families and started our trek northwest. Twelve families doesn't make a large wagon train, so we were small to begin with.

Then smallpox struck and some turned back. But we had nothing to turn back to, so we plodded on. When the disease hit, the wagons of the dead families had to be burned to stop the smallpox from spreading. But we picked up two extra mules, giving us two span to pull our wagon. We also had our two milk cows from the farm and a buckskin colt that we thought would be a mighty fine horse some day.

Ours wasn't a fancy wagon, just a converted buckboard. It was new when Mama and Papa were married and it had a single spring seat, with a tiny area for cargo behind. It still had the spring seat, but years ago Papa built a wagon bed and moved the spring seat nearer the front axle.

With the animals gone, we sat on the tongue of the wagon and cried. This was where we'd die. After we were cried out we started praying. At first we were accusing God for letting us down, but in time we were pleading with him, repenting of our deepest hidden sins.

Suddenly, as if an angel was sitting on the wagon tongue aside us, we felt better. So we'd die. What of it? Nobody gets out of this world alive. I wasn't afraid to die, but I had one regret. I guess it was a silly regret, but it was bothersome just the same—I'd never had a boyfriend. I mean a real boyfriend—one that would take me for a walk on a moonlit night and whisper sweet nonsense for me to adore. It seemed a shame not getting to have that experience.

Nothing better to do, Mama decided we should take stock of what was left. Our main source of food had been milk and cornmeal . . . before our cows were stolen. It's good eating, but I hankered for a little meat. We had had butter too, butter aplenty. Mama would put the cream in a bucket and hang it from the rear of the wagon as we traveled. By noon it would be butter and buttermilk. That, with the winter squash and cornmeal, tasted mighty fine.

With the cows stolen, we had dry cornmeal, winter squash, and nothin' else. Our water was almost gone, too. Water on the prairie is not hard to come by if you're on horseback. But on foot, water sources become almighty far apart.

At first we stayed with the wagon 'cause Mama had it in mind that since the men who stole our animals had happened along this area of the prairie, others would too. But we were fast learning that we were alone—*really* alone.

The day drug on and soon night arrived. Wondering what the next day would bring, I drifted to sleep under the wagon. During the night I was awakened by someone praying. It was Mama. I could see her out on the prairie in the starlight, a stone's throw from my bed, pleading for help.

A wave of irritation swept over me. God hadn't stopped Papa from joining the Confederacy and getting killed at

Shiloh. God hadn't kept the shysters from claiming our farm. He hadn't stopped our friends from dying of smallpox, nor had he stopped the horse thieves from stealing our animals and leaving us to die in this God-forsaken prairie.

Bitterly, I turned over. I don't know that I was all that angry with the Lord as much as I was confused. After all, what did I know? In a few days, possibly, I'd be standing before him, giving an account of myself . . . if'n he existed.

One sunset merged with the next and I lost track of how many days went by. As a family we'd taken to offering up some powerful prayers, but it was either our time to die or the Lord had forgotten us.

Mama put it to us, straight. "Do we stay here and die, or do we walk and die?"

"I'd rather walk," I said.

"Hector's legs are too short to walk far," she observed aloud, "but dying might be easier if he's worn out."

"I can walk good," Hector said.

"Yes, I suppose you can," Mama replied, tousling his hair.

We cleaned up as best we could and dressed in our best clothes . . . our dying clothes. Mama carried a light pot for cooking the corn meal, all the water we had left, and a picture of Pa. I carried a sack of cornmeal, and Hector carried the family Bible. And, believe it or not, we started off in good spirits.

All day we walked. There was no shade and though it was still spring, the sun was hot and heat waves danced above the grass. We found no comfortable place to stop, so we just plodded along, becoming a lazy partner in the heat-wave's dance. Sometimes I'd walk with my eyes closed, sometimes open. Often I stumbled, but who cared?

Once when I opened my eyes, I realized I'd fallen. Mama was sitting, cross-legged beside me, holding Hector and muttering an undisciplined prayer. Then she started singing, "Rock of Ages," but it sounded more like an Indian death chant than a hymn. I imagined Mama as an Indian squaw and almost laughed at the way she looked in my mind. Then, as if it was an apparition in the dancing waves, I saw an Indian sitting on a horse, watching us. I'm not a real believer in ghosts, but when you're dying, anything seems possible. I was disappointed that if there were ghosts, it was an Indian I saw instead of Papa comin' to take us to the other side. But considerin' all that's happened, it figured that God would pull something like this . . . if'n there was a God.

I struggled to focus my eyes but had a hard time. I figured things would be more clear after you were dead. But slowly, like when you're waking up from a dream, I came to realizin' that what I was seeing wasn't a ghost. It was a real Indian. His horse was stepping closer, and since I could hardly move, I just closed my eyes and waited for him to do whatever he was going to do to me. I'd heard some awful things about Indian treatment of captive women. Dying young was bad enough, but God wasn't even going to let me die in peace.

I could smell the horse now. Funny how your sense of smell increases when you're away from civilization. The smell of the horse was pleasant; it reminded me of Blueflower, a horse we had when I was little.

The Indian was standing over me now; I could smell him too. It wasn't the offensive unwashed smell of those men that stole our animals, but a fresh smell, like the earth and wind. I could also smell water.

He slid his hand under my head and lifted it. I played 'possum no longer but opened my eyes to take what was coming. I felt something touch my lips and then water entered my mouth. I swallowed, coughed, then took more water. It was the best tasting water I'd ever drunk, and cold, too. I'd heard that some Indians carry their water in wet skins, and as they ride the water gets cold enough to freeze your teeth. It was true.

I looked into his eyes—there was no expression there. His face was young and handsome, but emotionless. He pushed the skin of water to my mouth again, and I drank greedily. I would have drunk more but he pulled it away. Then he went to Mama and Hector and gave them water.

I studied him as he took care of Mama and Hector. He didn't look like any Indian I'd ever seen, but I wasn't sure why. I didn't detect an ounce of fat over his rippling muscles. Course he was nearly naked like most Indians are. I blushed as I stared at him in his leather loincloth and moccasins. But why should I blush? He wasn't a naked white man—just a savage. And what does it matter what a savage wears?

At his waist, hooked to the leather strap that held his clout, was a sheath knife—a white man's knife. Across his back was a quiver of arrows. A bow lay beside me. High on both arms were colorful arm bands, and around his neck was a bear's claw necklace.

Having given water to Mama and Hector, he again turned his attention to me. Since he didn't appear ready to scalp us, at least not immediately, I figured a gesture of friendship was in order.

"Me Mae," I said, hoarsely, pointing to myself. I wondered if he understood. His expression didn't change, but he lifted up my dress and ripped at my petticoat, tearing a large piece of material away.

This is it, I thought. I'm going to be raped. I gritted my teeth and closed my eyes but instead of any violence, I felt only the petticoat material being wrapped around my head. His hand came away bloody. I didn't even know I was hurt. I realized I had lost my bonnet.

"Me Mae," I said again, slowly. He just grunted and finished taking care of my head wound. The warrior was young. In fact he didn't look much older than me.

I looked into his eyes and thought I saw something . . . if I hadn't known he was Indian I would'a thought it was humor.

"Me Mae," I said for the third time.

"Hello, Mae," he replied. "Is English your second language?"

My jaw dropped. I'd heard very few Indians speak English and none who spoke it very good. This Indian sounded just like a white man.

"You can speak English?"

"Certainly, madame, and apparently you do, too."

I was embarrassed. "Are you Apache or Arapaho?" I asked.

"Neither. I'm Shoshone."

"I've never seen an Indian that looks like you. You're different."

"To be Shoshone *is* to be different," he replied, egotistically. "My name is Walking Short, but you can call me Billy, Billy Harold."

"Billy's an English name!"

"If you prefer, I also have a Ute name, but even in your quest for new languages, its pronunciation might confuse you."

I started to bristle. "Billy's fine with me," I said.

The horse stamped a hoof, and my eyes focused on Billy's Appaloosa mare. On its right flank was a red hand print, and below it was a symbol that looked like a keyhole. The horse carried a saddle, saddle bags, bedroll, and rifle. "I didn't know Indians used saddles." I said.

"I use a saddle," he said. " 'Cept when hunting or going into battle where they might get in the way. A white man's saddle is bulky, but it's comfortable and handy to tie gear to. And when I'm roping cows I need my saddle horn."

"You sound like a white man, and you have a white man's name, but you're Indian," I commented.

"That's right," he said, not answering my implied question.

"Mama has been praying for help for days," I said.

"Looks like he answered your prayers," Billy replied.

"I think God's a joker."

"Why?"

"Because he sent an Indian instead of an angel."

• CHAPTER TWO •

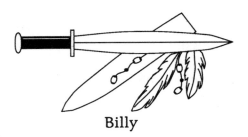

Billy

It could be I'm an answer to prayers, but all I know is that I'm just an Indian trying to be in harmony with nature and the Great Spirit.

Billy Harold's my name. It's a white man's name but I'm Shoshone. My Shoshone name is Walking Short. I have a Ute name, too, but I try to forget that.

My parents were killed in a raid by the Utes when I was eight years old, and I was taken slave. Shortly after I was entombed by the Utes to die as a grave tender, but that's another story.

I was rescued by a mountain man named Brigham Harold and became the adopted son of him and his young wife, Ermalinda. That, too, is another story. But Ermalinda's parents lived not far from the Texas panhandle, where I found the Brisk family.

Brigham Harold rescued me from the Ute grave and named me Billy. I've kind'a taken a liking to it. But I haven't forgotten the name my Shoshone father gave me.

My Shoshone father's relatives were all massacred by the Utes, but my Shoshone mother, Saw-wich, was from a different village. When I was growing up, my white father often took me to my mother's people to be trained as a warrior. He also taught me that the day would come when I would be needed to help my people adjust to the white man's world—a world they would be forced to live in.

But for the past three summers I have stayed away from the Shoshone 'cause they are making war on the white eyes, raiding along the Oregon Trail. Not only do I want to keep from being involved, but my white father wants me to stay away from all appearance of being involved. It was counsel that may have saved my life in January, a year ago. I was thinking of taking a load of corn to my mother's uncle, in Chief Sagwitch's band on the Bear River. My white father stopped me 'cause Sagwitch had chosen to fight the Black Coats. Had I not followed my White Father's counsel, I would have been in the Shoshone village when Colonel Connor's California Volunteers attacked, killing 300 villagers, maybe more.

I knew the white eyes' side of the story but still the massacre angered me fiercely. Chief Washakie, a great man of peace, spoke with me and counseled me to be temperate. He said when the wars were over I would be needed to help my people.

While I was growing up I had visited my Shoshone people every spring. But now that they were fighting the whites, I didn't go there anymore. I missed the visits sorely. When I heard my people had signed a peace treaty at Bridger I wasted no time in visiting again. Many tribal members were still bitter against the whites. They knew I lived with whites and called me a "white Indian." This hurt me deeply, but from their point of view I could see it was true. My white mother, Ermalinda, felt my pain. "It is always difficult being different," she said. "My parents have always accepted you. Why don't you visit them and give your people another season to cool down?"

I don't know that I really wanted to, but it seemed putting some distance between me and those who were angry with me would help so I soon started out for the Lloyds in Steady, Colorado.

I've lived nineteen summers, and I am now a man. As a man I have the right to communicate with the Great Spirit, the One-Above. In the life of an Indian there is only one inevitable duty—the duty of prayer. I felt a deep hunger in my soul and so went off alone into the prairie and fasted. I fasted and prayed for three days, as is the custom of my people—not a drop of food nor water passed my lips. I chanted the old chants passed down from generation to generation. Nobody knows what the words to the chants say, 'cept maybe the Shoshone Shaman. It's just a chant that gets you in tune with the One-Above, the sun, and the Four Old Men who direct the winds, rains, seasons, and the breath of life.

I wanted to speak with my father—not with Brigham Harold, though he is a mighty fine father—but with my Shoshone father, Jag-en-up, long since in the Happy Hunting Ground. Dressed in a leather clout and moccasins, I purified myself inside and out. I burned incense of cedar and sage and bathed in the smoke so that I could begin again.

In the white man's world, I'd gone through the teenage years and through school. Brigham Harold and Ermalinda were my guides then. In my Indian world, the men of the Shoshone tribe guided me through the rites of manhood to become a warrior. My white father had encouraged me to become a warrior. "You need both cultures," Brigham had said, "if you are to be an Indian in a white world."

I have a destiny—at least that's what Brigham says. My destiny is to save my people; to teach 'em how to survive the onslaught of the white eyes. The Shoshone Shaman saw my destiny as he peered into a mixture of badger and buffalo blood before a raid on the Utes when I was a child. It was enough to make a shaman jittery, so the raid was canceled. Then, years later while I was living with the Mormons in Manti, Brigham Young's Indian farmer saw my destiny in a dream and pronounced it a calling.

There is a big gap between the worlds of the Shoshone and the white eyes. I don't know if the gap can ever be breached. But there is one common thread . . . religion. Brigham Young says Indians have the old Hebrew religion, but that it is greatly distorted. He says Indians are the prayin'est folks he ever saw. I believe him, though Indians pray alone, having no organized religion. Fact is, there are about as many beliefs as there are people in each village, although the traditions of our fathers give us much common ground.

When a Shoshone brave wakes in the morning, he puts on his moccasins and steps down to the water's edge. There he throws handfuls of clear, cold water on his face or perhaps steps all the way in. After his bath he stands erect, facing the advancing dawn, and offers his silent orison. His mate may precede or follow him, but she doesn't accompany him. Each person must meet the Great Silence alone. As far as I know, all Indians do that or somethin' similar.

After three days' chanting, fasting, and praying, no vision came, and I was disappointed. On the fourth day I started back to the Lloyds' homestead feeling I had failed. I rode along chanting a somber chant, the way I remember my Shoshone father doing it.

When I topped the rise that overlooked the Lloyd homestead I reined my Appaloosa in short. Some distance directly ahead, an Indian stood, straight an' tall beside the trail—he was Shoshone.

Cautiously I nudged my Appaloosa forward, a feeling of excitement filling my chest. Even before I could make out his features, I knew it was him . . . my Shoshone father.

I rode closer and swung down, taking in my father's appearance. How often, especially during those captive months, I had longed to see him. He spoke not a word but pointed to the prairie.

I looked to the prairie where he pointed, but saw nothing. And when I returned my gaze to my father, he was gone. I'd had so many questions to ask him . . . and he was gone. The sting of not being able to see my father longer made it hard to blink back the tears. It's not that crying is unmanly. I'd seen tears in my father's dark eyes when my older sister died of the white man's disease, but I hadn't cried since I was a boy.

I stood there for a long time hoping he would come back but knowing he wouldn't. When I felt I could face Mrs.

Lloyd with dignity, I swung into the leather and rode on down to the homestead. Before I got there I put on my shirt and leggings 'cause Grandma doesn't like me to wear only a loincloth; white women are that way. She was framed in the door of her sod house, waiting for me. I rode up like a warrior should and swung down.

"Boy," she said, "you look like you've seen a ghost."

It troubled me that she could read me so well. "I've been fasting, Grandma, fasting and praying."

"Did it help?" she asked. She looked closely at me with her probing blue eyes and I knew I'd have to tell her.

"I saw my father—my Shoshone father. He pointed to the prairie."

"Did he say anything?" she asked.

"No," I said, swallowing hard. "But I think there's something in the prairie he wants me to see or do."

She was thoughtful, and when she spoke, she spoke very quietly. "You best do as directed," she said. "When are you going to leave?"

"As soon as I collect my rifle and gear."

"You do what you need to do, Billy, and I'll set some bread 'n milk 'n radishes on the table."

I turned to go.

"Billy?"

"Yes, ma'am?"

"I hear they keep'em busy on the other side. Doesn't give them much of a chance to chat." She smiled.

"Yes, ma'am," I said, and found I could smile back.

Bread and milk, and fresh radishes . . . it's a white man's meal and about the finest eating in the world, especially when you're hungry.

Thirty minutes later I swung into the leather and turned my horse's head to the southeast, into the prairie. As I didn't really know where I was going, I let the Appaloosa have its head feeling that the Great Spirit, or my father, would guide him. All alone there on the prairie I felt at peace, and yet there was the feeling that there was something I must see or do.

They were just specks out on the plains, about five miles past a creek, and I was mighty curious. I thought they were some kind of animals, and I checked the loads in my guns. But as I grew closer I saw they were people—two women and a child. I later learned it was the Brisk family.

Mae and Julienne were still and looked dead or dying. But Hector watched me through hollow eyes that revealed a mixture of fear and curiosity. He was clutching a Bible with such a firm hold you'd have thought he expected me to steal it.

I'd read the Bible. After all, I am a baptized Christian, baptized by Isaac Morley at the same time as Mama (Ermalinda, Brigham Harold's wife.) But I hold to the Great Spirit, too. Fact is, I worship the greatest power in the universe. When I'm with white folks I call that power God, and when I'm with the Indians I call that power the Great Spirit, One-Above, One Who Made All Things, or sometimes Ah-badt-dadt-deah, like the Crows. And I hold to all truth. Course, it's not always easy to tell what the truth is.

The truth was clear to me here, though. These people had lost their animals. They wouldn't have gotten this far across the prairie without any. They were in sore need of help and I was willing. Yet I was careful, 'cause sometimes white folks are almighty dumb. You try to help 'em, and they think you're a going to kill 'em. You can't turn your back on them. I s'pose Indians are the same way with white folks. It seems kind'a sad that human beings have given themselves such a bad reputation.

I gave 'em water, bandaged the girl's head, and pretty soon they came around. Then I fetched a ball of pemmican out of my saddle bag and sliced 'em off some. "Eat," I ordered. Hector and his mother ate like they were starved.

But the girl wouldn't eat. She just smelled the pemmican, and pushed it away. There was something about her that rubbed me the wrong way the minute I laid eyes on her. Oh, she was pretty enough, pretty as a picture, but she was surely a pilgrim.

"Eat," I ordered again, pushing the pemmican back to her.

"I don't want it," she said. "It's rancid!"

Pemmican is a ball of lean buffalo meat, pounded into a paste, mixed with suet and dried berries, and pressed into a cake or ball. Fat is something folks need badly. White folks who drink milk have plenty of fat, but these folks were living off corn gruel. Sure the pemmican was a little rancid. It had been made last fall when the berries were picked, but their corn meal didn't look at all good, either. It had weevils in it, and eating it would be a little like eating insects as do the Goshutes. She needed to eat and I wasn't in the mood to play games with her.

"Eat, or I scalp!" I ordered, putting my hand on the hilt of my steel knife. Her eyes grew big, and she started eating. Were it not for the Indian in me, I'd have broken out laughing.

We were only five miles from a lazy creek, but they were all done in, so where I found them is where we spent the night. The prairie looks flat but it isn't. There are ripples and wallows that do a good job of hiding a creek. The creek I had crossed five miles before reaching the Brisks was lined with cottonwood trees taller than the Tower of Babel. It was fifteen or twenty feet to the lowest branch. But it couldn't be seen from where we sat. The Brisks were a little awestruck when they realized they'd nearly died that close to water.

Come morning, we started for the creek. I used my riding horse for a pack horse. I set Hector among the bundles and gave the lead rope to Mae. When I told her to lead the animal she looked at me with fire in her eyes. I knew what she was thinking. White folks think Indians do their women wrong 'cause the women lead the animals and walk behind the men. But a man needs to have both hands free to use his weapons. He needs to look out for snakes and prairie dog holes and be far enough ahead so that he can spot an antelope or a buffalo and down the game before the chattering of the women and children drive the game away.

She didn't say anything; but even as far ahead as I was I could feel the fire in her eyes burning my back.

But I ignored it and let my ears fill with the sounds of the prairie and my nose fill with its sweet smell. A quarter of a mile from the creek I noted that the Appaloosa was pushing the women; her nostrils catching the smell of water. I also noted a growing roar. I searched the archives of my mind, digging through all I'd heard about the plains to place what was causing the rumble. I stopped so as to concentrate even harder.

When the women and Hector reached me, they, too, could hear the noise. In addition to the noise the prairie itself started trembling. To the southwest the horizon was dark and looked ominous.

"Is it an earthquake or a tornado?" Mae asked, her eyes flashing in terror.

"Neither," her mother replied. "It's a buffalo herd."

"I thought the days of the big herds were gone," Mae said.

"So did I," Julienne replied.

"Are they stampeding?"

"Probably not," Julienne answered. "More 'n likely they're just running. Your father said that sometimes the whole herd will run together sort of in step. When that happens it pulsates through the prairie, making an artificial earthquake."

As if on cue we started running toward the trees. Sure the trees were too large to climb quickly without a rope, but we ran toward them anyway. Seldom do you hear of a buffalo running into a tree, even in an all-out stampede. Fact is, I'd heard tell of buffaloes running upon Indian villages leaving them untouched. The head toros leading the herd open ranks at the last minute, swing out around the village, and close up once they are past the tepees. A person or animal out from the tepees will get trampled, but those in the tepees will likely be safe. Seems a buffalo doesn't know the difference between a tepee and a boulder.

We splashed through the creek and rushed to the thickest stand of trees we could find. We made our stand where four trees grew together. As the buffalo got closer, the trees started quivering, as did the water in the creek. Glancing over my shoulder I could see the lead toros a mile away, but the remainder of the herd was hidden in dust.

I returned to the creek with the horse and tried to get her to drink since I knew she should be thirsty. But she had other things on her mind, so I returned to the trees. I gave Mae my water skin and told her to fill it. She started to object, half out of oneriness and half out of not wanting to leave the safety of the trees; but before she could say two words, her mother grabbed the skin and raced to the creek. I turned my back on Mae and tied the horse securely to a tree with a lariat. I'd heard tell that domestic animals get caught up in the chase of a buffalo run and will join the herd.

Finally Mae began to catch the vision of what was taking place. She grabbed the Brisks' water bottle and cooking pot and raced to the creek for water. As if Thunder Bird himself flew overhead, the sky darkened and the roar of the herd turned to thunder. The herd was only a half mile away.

When Mae returned I pushed the horse's nose into the water. This time the Appaloosa drank, emptying the pot. I threw a blanket over her eyes and nostrils, and tied it loosely in place.

Then our time was up and the herd was upon us. Though I saw several toros, the vanguard runners were all cows, so I took it for an all-out stampede. In buffalo stampedes, the cows usually lead out.

They were huge creatures. Unlike our buffalo of the Rocky Mountains, these buffalo stood all of seven feet tall, even while running. With Hector in her arms, Julienne hugged a tree. Mae was confused and terrified. There was no fire in her eyes now. She just stood in the middle of the trees with her hands over her ears looking about ready to cry. Not really thinking about what I was doing I grabbed her, backed up to a tree, and held her tight. In truth, I was pretty terrified myself and it was good having someone to hang onto. Mae was a feisty girl, but she sure beat hugging a tree.

In the chaos of the stampede talking was out of the question. I had trouble even putting coherent thoughts together. I closed my eyes against the dust, buried my face in Mae's long hair, and felt the tremble of her body. As a defense against my fear I began chanting some chants of my youth. I could chant without thinking.

A quarter hour passed, and the thunder continued. Perhaps this was similar to what my people experienced when Christ first visited America. I wished for a bandanna to strain the dust from my eyes and lungs. I glanced up to check on the others. Julienne sat at the base of the tree with her skirt over her head, making a tent for herself and her son. Mae had her face buried on my shoulder, so again I buried my face in her long hair, and we made do.

An hour passed, and then two. It was surely a large herd. At times we thought we would die for lack of air, but the herd kept coming.

Finally the herd began thinning and some of my common sense returned. It seemed like a good time to harvest some meat. I half walked, half carried Mae to her mother and gently loosed her hold on me. For a moment it seemed kind of a shame to let go of her—it was the first time I had ever been that close to a girl.

My rifle was in its scabbard on the other side of the horse, but my bow and arrows were on my back. Though not a plainsman, I'd heard tell that huge toros brought up the rear of buffalo herds. They were almighty tough meat, and I wanted a blunt-horn—a buffalo young enough to be tender and large enough to make long strips of jerky.

Not wanting to miss the young buffalo, I quickly notched an arrow and waited for a good shot. When it came, I let loose and the arrow flew true. I was too close to miss anyway. The buffalo kept running, but I wasn't concerned. A buffalo will sometimes run fifty yards with an arrow in its heart. Twice more my arrows found their mark. I had faith that when the herd was gone, I'd find the animals' carcasses.

The last of the herd finally passed and there was a terrific silence. For a time it seemed we were deaf. But then I heard Mae and the others start coughing and I joined in with them. The creek was gone. Where it once flowed a mud bog remained. We would have liked to wash the dust from our faces and eyes, but we settled for a sip from our water bottles. With a damp cloth, I wiped the dust from my Appaloosa's nostrils.

Not far away, the buffalo carcasses awaited butchering. We washed up as best we could and set to work. Nobody much felt like talking so we didn't. I noticed Mae avoided my eyes, but that suited me just fine as we had a lot to do.

It doesn't take too long to butcher a buffalo, but it takes days for the meat to cure, though not as many as some folks think . . . a couple of good hot days will do it.

We cut thin, quarter-inch strips up to six feet long and set them in the sun to dry. We kept fires going to keep the flies away, though blow flies won't bother jerky once it starts drying 'cause the surface is too tough for the blow flies to penetrate.

Our work took a couple of days; but before we were through, the creek began to flow again. At first it moved thick and heavy like a mud slide, but later the water became clear and cool. It felt mighty good to take a long drink and to rinse the dust off our bodies.

I tried to get the Brisks to eat a large amount of the meat while it was fresh, but being white, they wouldn't eat much. Indians will go days without food, then stuff themselves when food is available. But white people eat just a little at a time, and eat three times a day. No sooner do you finish a meal, load up and start traveling, when white folks want to eat again. They spend all their time eating. Course, being raised since eight years old with whites, I've come to enjoy three meals a day, too. After eating three meals a day for a long time you are inclined to take food for granted. My Indian experience has taught me better than that.

We had far too much dried meat for my horse to carry, so in addition to the horse's pack we made a travois for the horse to drag. The only thing I dislike about travois is that they leave two long lines running through the prairie advertising your location.

But we started out one morning at first light. We kept near the creek as much as possible. The air was sweet and clear. Now and again, low in the west, you could see the purple mountains. Here and there prairie flowers gave color to Mother Earth, spreading their fragrance. Overhead the wide sky was broken by occasional puffs of white clouds and flying fowls looking for meals.

• CHAPTER THREE •

Mae

They called Mama "Widow Brisk" back in our wagon train. It's a title she didn't want. I never did fully understand just why Papa was so dead set on gallivantin' off to fight for the 'cause of the Confederacy. We weren't slave holders, and the war just wasn't worth losin' a Pa over.

Course the war wasn't over slavery to most of us; it was over being pushed around. No man likes to be pushed around, 'specially by them high-and-mighty Yanks. A man has to be a man or he ain't nothin', least that's what Papa always said. Course we all figured that with a show of force by the home boys them Yanks would give up and skeedadle back North, but they didn't.

Papa was one of them big, rawboned men that worked like a mule from can-see to can't-see. But come night he'd come in the house and take Mama in his arms. It made me feel so good to see two people in love. I can't imagine Billy ever treating a woman that way.

"Ma, may I run ahead and walk with Billy?" Hector asked.

"I don't think Billy wants anyone walkin' with him, else he'd be walking here with us instead of ahead, by himself."

"He's standoffish, if you ask me," I put in.

"I reckon he thinks he's just doing his job, Mae," Mama answered.

"Is Billy a good Indian?" Hector asked.

"I suppose he is," Mama replied. "Or we'd been missing our hair days ago."

"Back home the menfolk said the only good Indian was a dead Indian."

"Hector!" I said. I don't know why I said it, though.

"Do you love Billy?" he retorted.

"No!" I snapped. "What put that into your head?"

"You were holding him mighty tight during the stampede."

"Ma, make Hector shut up," I pleaded.

"Hector," Mama instructed. "White girls don't love Indian men. They're . . . different."

"What's different 'bout 'em?"

"I . . . I don't rightly know, Hector. Billy is the only Indian I've ever spoken with. But folks say they're different."

"Billy is surely different," I put in. Mama cast me a side-long glance. "What?" I asked, indignately.

"I didn't say nothin'," she returned. "See those clumps of mesquite, Hector?" she said, trying to change the subject."

"Yes, I see 'em," he said, eyeing me suspiciously.

"From now 'til we reach those mesquite, we won't say Billy's name, once! Okay?"

"I . . . I guess so. Do you know how the mesquite seeds got spread clear out here?"

"No, I guess I don't," Mama replied.

"Mustangs spread 'em."

"I don't get it," I said. "How can a horse spread mesquite? They grow from mesquite beans."

"Well," Hector began. "The horses eat the beans, but they don't digest 'em very well. Then they are soaked in the bowels of the horse, and when the horse drops 'em, they germinate."

"Who told you that?"

"Can't say."

"Why?"

"I ain't suppose to use his name 'til we reach the mesquite."

I grinned to myself, and we trudged along quietly, listening to the call of the prairie crane. I glanced at the sky, 'cause they say prairie cranes are the announcers of weather changes. The northwest sky was starting to blacken with clouds.

Ahead Billy was stopped, peering at something in the earth, waiting for us to catch up. We quickened our step, reaching him shortly.

On a gentle slope, half hidden in a clump of mesquite, Billy was hunched down by the remains of a wagon. Not a thing was left upright. The iron tires were just four circles in the spring grass. A well preserved hardwood ox yoke told us that the wagon had been pulled by oxen, rather than horses or mules.

I hunched down beside him and placed my hand almost reverently on the yoke. No doubt this represented someone's dream gone sour. Then I thought of our own wagon way back on the prairie.

We arose and began putting together a shelter. We pulled the tops of four mesquites together, forming crude protection against the approaching storm. Over the mesquites we anchored a couple of buffalo hides to turn the water. When that was completed we made a second shelter for the horse and gear.

• CHAPTER FOUR •

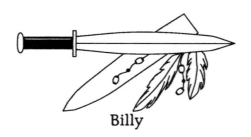

Billy

Leading the Brisks was a hefty burden. An enemy could come up at any time if I didn't stay alert. It ain't so hard taking care of yourself when you know what you're doing—but with two women and a boy? I stuck to the low areas and was careful when crossing ridges.

After ten days of travel we were a half day's ride from the town of Steady. That'd be at least a whole day since we were afoot. Several miles to the west, framed by the setting sun, we could make out a homesteader's shack. But we weren't going west, we were traveling north.

"My white grandparents live several miles straight ahead," I announced. "With good walking, we should reach their homestead in the morning before the sun is more 'n two hands high."

"Where were they from . . . before they took up homesteading?" Julienne asked.

"Virginia, I was told. Seems like half the West came from Virginia, or had kin that did."

"I was raised in Virginia, and so was Jedediah," Julienne admitted. "Knew a whole passel of Lloyd's when I was a young'un."

The next morning, Grandma and Grandpa Lloyd greeted the Brisks like long lost friends, and in time Grandma

Lloyd discovered she knew Julienne's old man, who was something of a mountaineer in Virginia. If'n they talked long enough, they might have even found they were kin . . . who knows? That night the Brisks camped down by the creek on a pretty spot where the creek runs along the Lloyd homestead border.

The next morning I dressed in white man's clothes and swung a blanket and saddle on my Appaloosa. Then, alone and sitting tall in the saddle, I cantered into the town of Steady.

It was flour I was after but a pack of trouble is what I found. The flour was for Ma Lloyd. With the extra mouths to feed she had run a little low. I was considering getting something for Mae, too. Though just a feisty, fifteen-year-old child, she stirred some strange feelings within me . . . feelings I didn't understand. When I held her in my arms as the buffaloes were running, I felt . . . protecting. Course she hadn't thanked me. More'n likely she'd claim she'd been protecting me.

Passing the public holding corral on my way to town, I pulled rein and studied the animals in the corral. There were two milk cows, a buckskin colt, and four mules. Two of the mules had a J B brand, the Brisks' brand back in Texas.

For a long while I brooded over pieces of the puzzle. As the public holding corral is used for holding animals brought from out of town to market, it seemed logical that even as I dallied, the thieves were dickering for a sale, probably at the general store.

Nudging my Appaloosa, I continued into town. Standing three legged in front of the general store were two handsome geldings wearing old saddles. I rode up beside 'em and swung down.

The Steady General Store was a false fronted building that did double duty for a post office. In front was a combination porch and boardwalk lined with weathered wicker chairs. Come winter, the chairs were carried inside to circle the potbellied stove. They were being held down by several townsmen, the usual crowd.

"Noticed some mules down at the holding corral," I commented.

"So there are, but what's it to you, Injun?" The speaker was a paunchy man who spoke with a New England twang.

"Careful, Alex. That's Brigham Harold's boy," a second man said, quietly. Alex's expression froze, then his Adam's apple bobbed.

"The owners are dickering inside with Mr. Lassanger," Alex gestured, almost as an apology.

"More 'n likely they're dickering for the sale of the animals in the corral," I stated.

"Wouldn't know."

It's always good to get public sentiment on your side before you start something, so I gave an explanation. "I found a widow with two children abandoned out on the prairie and brought them to the Lloyd homestead. They said five horse thieves stole their animals. The animals in the corral wear the J B brand, which I suspect belongs to the widow's old man, Jedediah Brisk."

The men exchanged glances. Horse thieving is a serious offense. Stranded without horses can mean death. Horse thieves are usually hung with no questions asked. I stepped into the store. It smelled of leather goods with a faint odor of gun oil mixed in. From the bodies of two drifters came the stench that comes of a bath long needed. They were dickering with Lassanger, the store proprietor, postmaster, and town mayor.

"That's not much for two fine looking milk cows," one drifter was saying. He was dressed in rags, or nearly so.

"That's true," Lassanger said. "But . . ." He didn't finish what he was going to say, yet I knew what was concerning him. It just didn't seem right for a couple of drifters to be roaming around the country with a couple of milk cows. So I spoke right up, and informed him.

"They stole 'em, Mr. Lassanger. Stole 'em from a widow with two kids. I found the widow and kids wandering out on the prairie half dead and led 'em in. The widow's late husband was Jedediah Brisk and the cows, the colt, and two of the mules are sporting a J B brand."

All eyes went to me, and it was clear I'd caught the thieves red-handed. The drifter's eyes were hard and cruel. "You're lying, Injun!" one said. Then turning to Lassanger asked, "You a-going to take the word of an Injun over a white man?"

"Well now, I know this Indian and his word is worth listening to."

The man swung at me. I blocked his swing, stepped into him, and rolled him off in a hip roll. He recovered quickly and came at me again. This time I met him with a hard blow to the heart, and it surprised him. He'd never seen an Indian use boxing techniques. But Brigham Harold was really something with his fists—said they kept you from having to kill your opponent—and he had taught me a few things.

He landed a right hook that jarred me to my toes. Numbly I blocked a second punch. Then I stepped close to him, elbowed him in the ribs, and kneed him where it hurt. He bent over in pain. I might have quit there had I not remembered the dying bodies of the Brisks when I found them. So I put my knee in his face. I felt crushing bones and knew I'd broken his nose. He sat down hard.

"You should o' listened," Lassanger drawled as he covered the two drifters with a shotgun, "when I warned you that the Indian was Brigham Harold's boy."

The man named Alex spoke from the door. "You say the animals were stolen from a widow and two young'uns?" I looked him in the eyes and thought I saw a believer.

"Yes. They're camped on the creek, on the edge of the Lloyd homestead," I replied.

The horse thieves were sweating it, they surely were, 'cause in Steady there is no jail. All it takes is a town trial and a necktie party down at the cottonwoods.

"Pete," Lassanger directed, "you and Alex go down and fetch the widow. You can take my buggy." Then, turning to the drifters, he asked, "You got names?"

"I'm Tex and he's Smith."

"Pretty nondescrip names, I'd say. Are they the names you want written on your shake?" Lassanger was speaking of a rough shingle used as a tombstone and inscribed with an epitaph.

"What's all this talk about a shake?" Tex put in. "Smith and I were just following orders, working for the brand. It wasn't our idea to take the critters. Just let us go and you can have the animals. We don't want nothing for 'em."

"Then you admit the animals are stolen?" Lassanger asked.

"Yes, but it wasn't us who stole 'em. It was Harry, our boss."

The townsmen in the room gave each other a knowing look, then Lassanger turned to me. "Billy," he said, "this town has business, and we want you out of it. Pete and Alex need to be here, so you take my buggy and fetch the Brisk family to claim their livestock." I knew what they were going to do. Frontier justice is always swift.

I drove Lassanger's buggy to the Brisks' camp. When I drove up, Julienne looked at me curiously. "Came out to fetch you," I said. "Mr. Lassanger, the storekeeper, sent me."

"Didn't know anyone knew we were here," Julienne replied. "I always like going to town, but what's going on?"

"We're a-going to get some stock to pull your wagon, ma'am."

She hesitated. "We don't have money . . . nothing to pay for stock, 'cept our own labor." I knew what she was thinking. A woman can only earn fifty cents a day, top wages. A fair wagon and ox team cost $184. Good Missouri mules, the type stolen from them, cost $80 a span when they could be had but they usually couldn't be had at any price.

"Just come on, and let's go," I replied, helping the womenfolk into the buggy. Then I clicked to the team, and moved 'em out. A good teamster can click his tongue so loudly that it sounds like a whip crack. I'm not the best teamster in the world, but I can hold my own.

As we neared the holding corral, on the near side of town, Mae gasped. Dangling from the crosspole of the corral gate were the bodies of the two horse thieves, Tex and Smith. With their hands tied behinds their backs, they were suspended by their necks in the traditional, thirteen loop hangman's noose. They were quite dead.

"Look Mama!" Mae squealed. So occupied with the sight of the hanging horse thieves, Julienne hadn't noticed the animals in the corral.

"It's Bossie and Bellie!" Hector yelled in delight. "And those are our mules, too."

Julienne threw me a questioning look, and I spilled the story. "I had no idea they'd hang the thieves right here on the corral gate," I concluded. "But it's a western custom to physically attach the punishment to the crime." A paper was pinned on Tex's shirt. It read, "They won't steal no more mules."

We rode on into Steady, where Julienne officially claimed her property. Then we returned to the corral and, under the feet of the hanging horse thieves, hazed the livestock out and drove 'em home.

All the way back to the Brisks' camp, my mind wandered to the three remaining horse thieves. I hadn't one iota of evidence where they might be. The Brisks filled me in on their descriptions, and Tex had said the boss's name was "Harry."

"Julienne," I asked. "You said the horse thieves were down from the Nation. Why do you think they were from there?"

"They came from the northeast," Julienne explained. "They had a Northern accent, and they drove the stolen animals southwest."

"Then why did the animals turn up in Steady, to the northwest from where they were stolen?"

"I've been thinking about that, too," she replied. "Maybe they changed directions to avoid the buffalo stampede. It came out of the southwest."

• CHAPTER FIVE •

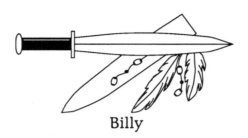

Billy

A good horse under me, and the wind in my face, I set out in the pre-dawn darkness. Behind me trailed the four Brisk mules. My destination was the wagon on the prairie—the Brisks' wagon.

Alone, but not lonely, I rode along nice and easy—I enjoy my own company. Fact is, I feel sorry for folks who don't enjoy being alone at times. Course you're never really alone when you have a good horse to talk to.

I rode into the dawn, letting my mare set her own pace. She liked to travel—born, I suspect, with wanderlust in her veins. She was the horse for me.

Dawn wasn't full grown, but I could see well enough. I kept the creek to my right and traveled several miles in peace, but then I caught a whiff of smoke. The smell was only there for a moment, then it was gone.

The smoke made me almighty curious, for in the back of my mind I'd been brooding over the whereabouts of the three remaining horse thieves. This is a big country, but there are few people. It's easier to hide in a town or city than out here.

I rode as warily as I could for being in the wide open while anxiously looking for cover. A mile farther along I found the spot I was looking for—a tiny grassy area secluded by trees. There I picketed the mules and doubled back to vent my curiosity.

After half a mile I swung down to proceed on foot. In my moccasins I could move noiselessly. I ground hitched my mare and was about to move out when I saw her swell her side in preparation for a whinny. I clamped my hand across her nose and stifled her whinny. Fearful she would give away my position, I moved her a quarter mile back and left her tied to some willows.

Since most white men are about as silent as a herd of buffaloes, finding their camp was not hard. There were three men, all nursing cups of steaming liquid. It wasn't coffee, as the aroma of coffee carries well on the breeze. More 'n likely it was herb tea or a coffee substitute. I inched closer, wanting to catch their conversation.

"I'm sick of bean coffee!" one man said.

"You never were long on patience, Mel. Just hold on. Tex and Smith should return soon."

"They're long overdue. Do you suppose something has gone wrong?"

"Tex is salty and can handle himself, though I sometimes wonder about Smith. Anyway, if you hadn't lost your cool down in Texas and killed that deputy, we'd a'sold them mules long ago and be eatin' high on the hog now."

"It wasn't my fault, Harry, and you know it. The deputy was on to us, saying honest drifters don't have milk cows for sale. I told ya we should a' killed 'em for beef."

"It's coffee we want, not beef . . . coffee and real side pork and sugar."

"Ever wonder what happened to the widow and young'uns we left out on the prairie?"

"That's enough of that kind of talk, Mel. More 'n likely they're long since dead, and we did 'em a favor, 'cause they'd have died anyway."

I'd heard enough, so I backed out. They'd have a surprise coming, as Tex and Smith weren't a-going to return, and they had a spell longer to go before they ate store bought food. I made my way to my Appaloosa and swung into the leather. When I got to where I'd picketed the mules, they were ready to travel.

I rode southeast the morning through and on into the afternoon. In my knapsack was cornbread and cold chicken. I ate well. When that was gone I'd live on jerky or kill me some fresh meat, whichever I fancied at the time.

On into the evening I rode, letting the Appaloosa set her own pace. By noon the third day I was to the place where I'd first found the Brisks nigh onto three weeks ago. Looking at the spot where I'd forced Mae to eat made me think of her. Angry with myself, I shook those thoughts out of my head. What was I doing? Mae was just a child, although the way she was startin' to fill out her dress foretold she was nearly a woman.

It wasn't too difficult figuring out where they'd left their wagon. If the Brisks had walked a straight route, it'd be to the southeast, not many hours' ride. They thought they'd walked a straight route, but who knows? White folks tend to wander with the sun's journey across the sky.

Two hours later I located the wagon. But it had guests: prairie mice. The mice had been attracted to the wagon by the sacks of cornmeal inside. Nearby was a large rattler, sunning itself and waiting for one of them prairie mice to come close.

I lay claim to the wagon and the rattlesnake too. Rattlers are good eating. Texas rattlers aren't like the Great Basin rattlesnakes of Utah. The Great Basin rattler is an easy going, lazy snake that will hide in a crack in the trail, and allow a hiker to step over it. But some Texas rattlers will chase you if'n you irritate them. Folks in Texas aren't as likely to kill a rattler with an irrigation shovel. Most Texans stand ten feet away and blast the rattler apart with a shootin' iron. It all seems a waste of ammunition to me. Indians will likely as not sneak up and snatch the snake behind the head, 'cause they're practiced in agility. If'n they're not agile enough to snatch the rattler, chances are they won't live to have any children. I just limbered up my knife-throwing arm and let my modified Arkansas toothpick fly.

Pa, my white mountain man father, observed that few Indians have the background to appreciate the white man's fine weapons. But when you combined an Indian's trained agility with white man's balanced weapons, he said it's a combination hard to beat. Still . . . there are very few Indians that become good with white man's weapons even after they acquire them.

I severed the rattler's head just as pretty as you please, and the snake started it's coiling and twitching routine. A snake is like a chicken, which runs around on reflex action long after it's head is severed. If you get too close to a severed snake's head you're likely to get bit. So after killing a snake, you bury it's head. As you're skinning the reptile it still rattles now and again, making you think a second rattler is ready to strike.

I started a fire and roasted the rattler. Rattlesnake is tender when fried or stewed, but roasted it's rather tough. It's like eating a chicken neck, except the bones are softer, and you can chew them. You can dine on one large rattler all afternoon as you ride along.

The wagon was a covered buckboard made of oak, with a few pine planks. At one time it had seen a coat of black paint. The wheels had been painted orange. Ten years ago, black, blue, and orange were the most popular colors for wagons. But nowadays folks favor green wagons with yellow wheels. Some wagons are painted with ox blood, or a mixture of ox blood and skim milk. It's a poor man's paint, but it does the job. I'd have to speak to the Brisks about getting a fresh coat of paint on their wagon before the wood started to rot.

The wagon was not heavy enough to require two span of mules, but I had 'em, so I hitched 'em. The two mules carrying the J B brand submitted well to harness. But the other two needed training. I hitched the semi-trained team nearest me, so my whip could touch 'em.

When whipping up a well-trained team, you don't often strike 'em with the whip, but crack it near their ears instead. Course a good mule skinner can take the hide right off a mule with a whip if he takes a mind to. But it's not a very good idea, 'cause it doesn't make points with an employer since mules are valuable property. You can move out a well-trained team with a click of your tongue and the ripple of the reins. Course you keep the whip handy for the dogs that take a mind to chase your team.

I put a halter on my mare and tied the end of the halter rope to the rear of the wagon. Then I whipped up the team and after a few miles all four mules were pulling together. I fired a pistol shot past the teams' ears. It was a training measure, as a gun-shy team can give you problems. If the team had started running, I'd have allowed them to tire themselves out, then repeated the training until the team was used to guns. But this team didn't seem too gun shy. The report of the gun startled 'em, but they didn't run.

When driving a covered wagon, you can't see behind you. That bothered me, so I routinely peered around the edge of the canvas. To be alone astride a horse is one thing. But to be alone with a team and noisy wagon is something else. I checked the load in my weapons and drove on.

Come night, I camped in a large bowl. Shoshone warriors are taught to set up a light camp, prepare their meal, then move on before sleeping. Course it would do me no good to move on with the wagon and all, so I'd taken to setting up a light camp but sleeping fifty yards away. I thought I was prepared, but when company came that night it nearly caught me by surprise.

They came out of the night, three of 'em. When they left, there were only two. They came in quietly enough, but quietness is what saved my bacon. They weren't moving slowly enough for the insects to get accustomed to them, and insects make a sound all their own.

Not knowing why, I awakened. I was about to roll over and fall back to sleep but then I realized I couldn't hear the usual night noises. I remained motionless and by and by I saw three black forms creep into camp. I didn't know who they were, but I knew they were not friends. Friends would have stood up and yelled, "Hello the camp!" You never walk right up to anyone's camp without hollering first . . . it just ain't polite, and it can get you killed.

I fit an arrow into my bow and watched my chances. As a man was about to pull the mule's picket pins, I let the arrow fly. He let out a startled cry and clutched his chest. The other two men didn't know what to think, but they knew what to do. They faded out of my camp in seconds. Indians are not big on night fighting, so when you see an Indian arrow flying out of the dark you can bet the Indian is sure of himself.

Come first light, I examined the dead man. He was one of the horse thieves, the only one I hadn't been able to brand with a name. I stripped the body and scalped it according to Indian tradition. Since becoming Brigham Harold's son, I usually had no use for a scalp. In the Indian world you can proudly display your scalps, but in the white world nobody wants to see them. However, my purpose in counting coup was to make it look like an Indian attack. It would keep the horse thieves guessing, trying to figure out what was going on. I also had a hunch a scalp might come in useful sometime.

I moved the team out, setting a rapid pace. At first I thought the rapid pace was to set as much distance between me and those men as possible, but as I rode I realized I was a little anxious to get back to the Brisks— especially to Mae. It was a thought I didn't like . . . I mean I liked it, but I didn't like it. In my whole life I'd never courted a girl, and this was not the time to start. I'd no call to even think of her. Besides, I was about to return to Utah, and the Brisks were going on to Oregon. I sorely needed to get them out of my head.

I could have made it back to the Lloyd's homestead that evening, but as I passed a bed of white clay I decided to dally long enough to clean my clothes. I rubbed the white clay into my leggings, clout, and buckskin shirt, and brushed 'em good. It's the best way I know to clean 'em. When I'd finished, they were not only clean but a shade or two lighter. Course I wasn't cleaning up to impress Mae . . . no siree. I was cleaning up 'cause that's the proper way to keep yourself . . . clean.

• Chapter Six •

Mae

At my age, nearly sixteen, many girls are married and keeping house. There I lay, in the still of the predawn darkness, listening to Billy as he prepared to leave on his journey to retrieve our wagon. There was a longing in me as I listened to him go. I peeked out of my covers but could see nothing. Billy intrigued me. He was an Indian all right, but he was so strong and good looking. Many white people call Indians savages. Billy doesn't seem very savage. Yet he doesn't come across as warm and friendly either. He always walked ahead of us and stayed aloof as if he were better than us. But then he had saved our lives, and sometimes when he looked at me . . . but that's ridiculous 'cause he's an Indian.

I wondered if the wagon would be gone when he got there. Maybe Billy would never return. Many things can claim a man's life. He could break a leg and get blood poisoning, get caught in a buffalo stampede, get himself set upon by outlaws, or catch smallpox. Sometimes men ride out and you never hear of them again. But why do I care? He's an Indian.

"Mae, do you love Billy?" Hector asked again, as I looked to the southeast prairie come mid-day.

"What makes you ask such silly questions?" I said coldly.

"Mama said you were old enough to fall in love."

For a moment I thought of how tenderly Billy had held me during the buffalo stampede. He had put his face in my hair. Course, where else could he have put it?

"Well, I'm not!" I said. "Billy is just a . . . savage!"

"Billy isn't a savage, he's a Christian Indian."

What Billy could be sometimes was cantankerous and downright stubborn; but then again Ma said I was that way too.

We were working in the Lloyds' field, trading labor for garden vegetables. Thanks to Billy we had plenty of buffalo meat. Thanks to Billy we were alive. Thanks to Billy we had our animals back. Thanks to Billy . . . it went on and on. I wasn't sure I liked having to be so thankful to Billy.

Our camp, on the banks of the creek, wasn't much of a camp, just a wickiup and a fire ring. When Billy returned we'd have our wagon again and we'd have a real camp. Yet he'd return just to be gone again. But that's the way it should be.

High noon on the eighth day Mama, Hector, and I were resting in the shade of a mulberry tree munching on mulberry leaves. Faintly we could hear the jingle of a wagon in the distance. It sounded like our wagon.

I'm not saying that every wagon has it's own sound, but a buckboard sounds different from a Conestoga or a buggy. And both sound different from one of those heavy two story, ox drawn wagons. The two story wagons have a luggage space below a riding bed. The riding bed often has a tiny castiron stove, bolted to the floor, with a stove pipe up through a ring in the canvas.

As we listened, the jingle of a buckboard filled our ears . . . you could hear the tiny squeak of the spring seat. Our eyes went to the bend in the road, where we caught our first glimpse of the wagon.

It *was* ours!

I knew it wasn't ladylike, but when the buckboard rounded the bend I started running toward it. Hector kept pace with me. Though it shamed me, I realized it made me happier to see Billy again than our wagon. As I neared the wagon Billy pulled rein, maybe a little harder than he intended, and the wagon bucked to a stop.

Placing one foot on a wagon spoke, Hector vaulted to the seat. Then he did something awful, just awful. He threw his little arms around Billy and hugged him as if he were Papa. That was like Hector, too innocent to realize that Billy wasn't one of us, but an Indian. Billy looked at me from over Hector's shoulder and I felt myself blushing. That made me angry. I had no reason to blush. "We're glad you're back," I said, a little distantly.

"Are you glad I'm back 'cause I returned or because your wagon returned?" he kidded.

Quick-as-a-wink I replied, "It's because our wagon has been returned, of course." For some reason he laughed. It was the first time I'd heard him laugh and it sounded nice.

By then Mama had reached us and she was beaming. It had been so long since I'd seen her that happy. I just stood there, enjoying her good pleasure as she exchanged greetings with Billy. Then she took her place on the wagon seat beside him, and I climbed in the back with Hector, and we rode to our camp.

In the back of the wagon was an ox yoke. It was weather beaten, but made of fine hard wood. It was the yoke we'd seen weeks earlier out on the prairie. At camp, Billy pulled out the yoke as Mama eyed it, inquiringly.

"I thought of a way you could get enough provisions to last you all the way to Oregon," Billy explained. "You could sell your mules and buy oxen."

"What do you suppose the mules would bring?" Mama asked.

"Because of the war, mules are scarce. They could bring you forty dollars a head in trade, but you're not likely to get much cash money, as cash is scarce, too. Oxen will cost you half that, and you'll only need one yoke of 'em."

It was a thing to consider. A hundred twenty dollars in trade is a lot of money, more than we'd seen in many a year.

However, at fifty cents a pound for potatoes and ten cents a pound for prime beef, we'd have to spend the money wisely to make it last.

"Do you think we can find a company to travel with along the Oregon Trail?" Mama asked.

"If you get to the Oregon Trail before mid-summer, you'll have no problems."

"There is a nine-wagon train in town from Texas," Mama commented.

"What are their teams?"

"Horses and mules."

"If you exchange your mules for oxen, you won't be able to keep pace with 'em. If you keep your mules, you won't have money for enough provisions for the journey," Billy observed.

"Oxen may not be able to keep up with mules, but we won't be too far behind and can catch up each evening."

Later that evening I saw Billy sitting by the creek sharpening his knife on a stone. I fiercely wanted to ignore him but it was like my eyes were magnets in a compass and he was the North Pole. Papa always told me that when you have a problem you best meet it head on. I wanted to talk to Billy so I figured I'd just go over there and do it. But when I got to the bank above him I lost my nerve and just stood there. I thought maybe he would look up and invite me to sit beside him but the only thing he was noticin' was the edge of his blade.

It made me mad that I couldn't ignore him like he could me. I picked up a large flat stone and threw it into the creek just in front of him. It landed closer than I had intended and got him mighty wet. Now I would've gotten all red in the face had someone done that to me, but without even looking up he just said, "Usually I just spit a little on my stone when it needs a little moisture."

I didn't wait for an invitation any longer but just slid down the bank and plopped down beside him. "Is it because you're an Indian that you're so rude or is it just 'cause you're Billy?" I asked, not even trying to hide my anger.

I immediately felt bad because although his face was stone I saw hurt cross his eyes.

"What do you think?" he asked. He looked me straight in the face. Although feeling guilty I met his dark eyes bravely. I didn't see an Indian, just Billy—a young man doing the best he could in a tough world.

Now it's against my nature to apologize 'cept when Mama makes me, but there's no denying I owed him one.

"Guess I'm the rude one," I said.

I believe I saw him smile for an instant, but then he said, "If'n you were a squaw and threw that rock I'd have to roast you over a fire in front of the whole camp to get my honor back."

Because of that hint of a smile I didn't believe him, but I didn't tell him so. With greetings over with we just sat in silence. He sharpened his knife and I stared into the creek. Finally I spoke. "What are you going to do?"

"About what?" he asked.

"Are you going to stay here in Steady, or are you going back to Utah?"

"Utah is my home, Mae. It's time for me to go home."

After he said that I figured it was time for me to go, too. I didn't want to leave, but suddenly I wasn't feeling very well.

Come night, I lay awake in my blanket roll long after the others were asleep. I watched Scorpius in the heavens, and was looking for Orion, the Hunter, but then remembered that you don't see Orion this time of year. Before long I saw Billy's face in the stars and I started crying.

Movement caught my eye, and I turned to see Mama sitting beside me. Embarrassed I dried my eyes on the blankets.

"What's wrong, Mae?"

"Nothing."

"Nothing?"

"No . . . nothing."

"Mae," she urged. "There must be at least one thing that's bothering you."

"It's nothing, Mama."

She didn't reply, but drew herself closer, and took me in her arms as if I were a little girl. We watched Scorpius together.

"Mama," I said after a while. "Why do we have to go to Oregon?"

"They say the soil in Oregon is so rich that tomatoes grow the size of pumpkins," Mama replied. "There are so many folks in Oregon that are hunting for gold and so few farming that you can get rich from growing produce and selling it to the gold hunters, or so they say."

"Maybe they are just yearnings, Mama. Maybe tomatoes don't grow that big. And maybe by the time we get there, the gold mines will have played out."

"Maybe they are just yearnings, Mae. But we've lost our farm in Texas and have no place to live, 'cept in the wagon. As long as we have to start over, why not start over in Oregon?"

"Why not Manti?" I replied.

"There is nothing in Utah, Mae. Utah is for the Mormons. They're not like us."

"The Greer family, that came to Texas with their Negro slaves . . . they were like us, weren't they?"

"Yes, they were like us, but most Mormons aren't like them. Most Mormons are holier-than-thou abolitionists, or so they say."

"What about Billy?"

"Billy isn't like us either, him being an Indian."

"Mama, is there *anybody* that's *like* us?"

• CHAPTER SEVEN •

Mae

I know that Mama, being a widow, was often lonely. But Billy seemed to make things easier and she learned to rely on him. With his help, she traded the four mules to Mr. Lassanger for two oxen and one hundred twenty dollars worth of provisions. The oxen were gentle animals but had not been under yoke. Neither Mama nor I had driven oxen, so we took lessons in ox driving from Mr. Lassanger. Much to our chagrin, the lessons were given at the town holding corral with all the town loafers watching and enjoying the spectacle.

Two burly men yoked the team together, but even yoked together the oxen tried to take every direction but forward. It took the two men, pushing and shoving, to jockey the animals into position on each side of the wagon tongue. Then getting the oxen to pull together took the two men, one on each side of the team, prodding 'em along. They say training oxen is largely a matter of letting the animals know what is expected.

There is not always logic to the decisions you make in life. As badly as Mama wanted to reach the Oregon Trail, she was leery of being a lone family on the trip, even if we could attach ourselves to an established company. So she approached Billy and solicited his help.

"Will you accompany us at least as far as the Oregon Trail?" she asked. "It's as short a route to Utah as any, and we need you."

"Yes," he responded, quietly.

Billy didn't know that Mama had told me he had consented to come with us. While I was busy working over the fire, preparing the evening meal, Billy walked up and started talking to me. It kinda made me feel good to have him speaking to me, but I didn't let it show.

"Your mother has invited me to accompany your family at least as far as the Oregon Trail," he said.

"What did you answer?" I asked, putting a little arrogance in my voice. Mama, who was mendin' one of Hector's shirts, was listening in. She had heard my tone of voice and looked at me like I could use a could use a paddlin'.

"I said I would go with you," Billy replied, in a neutral tone.

"Why?" I asked. I couldn't help myself.

"I . . . I . . . ," Billy stammered.

"I guess we do need help milking the cow," I answered him.

"No ma'am," Billy answered, that neutral tone turning a little sharp. "But you might lag behind the rest of the company," he said at last, "and would need a man around in case something happened."

"I suppose if something's going to happen, you'd be as good a man to have around as anybody," I said. For once I had got the better of him. But as he walked away, I didn't feel all that proud.

The next morning a boy from town appeared at our camp. "Have a message from Mr. Lassanger," the lad said. "There's a mule train in town on it's way to Laramie. Says he can get you attached to the train, if'n you're willing to tag along behind the mule skinners."

"Tell Mr. Lassanger that we're willing," Mama said. "Tell him that we'll be right in."

The train was made up of three heavy freight wagons bound for Laramie, each pulled by three span of mules.

Behind the freight wagons were six wagons of gold hunters pulled by fine horse teams. The gold hunters were family men with their families, bound for Oregon. They had attached themselves to the freight wagons for security. They, too, planned on joining a westward bound company once they reached Laramie.

The wagon master, a man named Stanley Jackman, was a big man with a cantankerous streak. He only accepted us as members of the train because he owed Mr. Lassanger a favor.

Mr. Jackman didn't like us, I could tell. "You'll keep up or be left behind!" he declared. We expected nothing less.

"Who's the Injun?" he asked, looking to Billy. "What's he doing here?"

"He's with us," Mama stated.

"I'll not have an Injun along!"

"His name is Billy Harold, adopted son of Brigham Harold," Lassanger put in. At the time I didn't know it, but Stanley Jackson's wife had been killed by Indians, and he held all Indians responsible. Yet the name of Brigham Harold seemed to work magic.

"Knew Brigham," Jackman said. "Fine fighting man . . . but I won't have an Injun in my company."

Billy's face was stoic, but I'm sure he was hurt.

Lassanger shuffled uneasily, studying the ground. The air was tense, and for a long time no one spoke. Then Lassanger broke the silence.

"Had any Indian trouble?"

"Nope."

"Expectin' any?"

"I always expect Injun trouble."

"Billy is a tame Indian and can save your life in the clinches."

"Yes but . . ."

"It's only for a couple of weeks at the most. And you owe me a favor, Stanley."

Billy was sauntering off in disgust, apparently fed up with the Stanley Jackmans of this world. Jackson was thoughtful, weighing the words carefully.

"Okay," he said. "I'll take him and the widow family along, but only 'cause I owe you one."

• CHAPTER EIGHT •

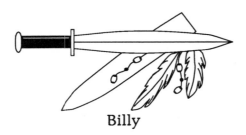

Billy

I'm just an Indian, without a whole lot of experience with wagon trains, 'cept for Mormon companies in Utah Territory. Still, I know that normally wagon masters rotate the positions of the wagons in their train. Each morning the drag wagon becomes the lead wagon, then the next day it is second in line, and so forth. But Jackman kept his three mule team at the front of the line, every day. Likewise, he kept the Brisks' ox team in the rear.

There were times on the gradual downhill stretches that we were a full mile or so behind the wagon train, but on the uphill stretches we always caught up. Oxen plod much at the same pace up or down grade, and the Brisks didn't have much to weigh down their wagon. They didn't even have a plow, as most of their possessions had been taken when they lost their farm back in east Texas.

So we rode along in the dust of the wagon train . . . when we were able to keep up. Like a cowboy riding drag behind a cattle herd, we each wore a bandanna over our mouths and noses. But on downhill stretches, the Jackman teamsters would whip up their teams and we'd be left behind to enjoy relatively dust free air.

Then came the day when we were so far behind that all we could see was the dust of the wagon train in the distance. Jackson was showing us no mercy a-tall. We nooned by ourselves.

"Think we'll catch up by tonight?" Julienne asked. She was nervous at being left alone, as she ought to have been.

"More 'n likely," I replied. "With that cloud o' dust, we ain't likely to lose 'em. You can see where they are for nigh onto ten miles."

"How far behind are we?"

"Three, maybe four miles," I replied.

"I bet if we really whooped up these oxen we could catch up," interjected Hector.

"I think they done lost most of their desire to run," I answered.

"Why's that?" he asked.

I was saved from answering by Julienne's "Never mind, Hector."

"They must be moving," Mae observed. "The dust plume is higher than it was a short time ago."

Mae's comment caught me by surprise because I thought they had been moving the whole time. I looked closer and saw the blackness of smoke mixed with the dust.

"They're under attack! That's smoke!" I cried.

Of one mind, we ran for the oxen that had been unyoked for our noon rest. With everyone's help, including Hector's, we yoked the team and pulled the wagon into a small arroyo seeking a place to hide.

With the wagon secured, we crawled to a vantage point and watched the surrounding prairie. We saw nothing but the smoke. After several hours the smoke began dying down so I mounted my Appaloosa and cautiously began a scouting expedition.

After riding in overlapping circles, I found where many unshod horses had waited. It had been an ambush with more than fifty Indian braves involved. I approached the smoldering train from the same cover the Indians used when they ambushed.

All the horses and mules were gone, which I had expected. The teamsters were dead and scalped, their naked, disemboweled bodies gleaming in the afternoon sun. I noticed there were very few bodies of women and children. The first of the buzzards had already started feeding. They say that buzzards won't feed until the odor of decay drives them wild with hunger, but they're wrong.

All the wagons had been looted and set a-fire. Some had been burned to the ground, but mostly the canvas and contents had been burned. Wagon canvas burns especially quickly 'cause it has often been oiled or waxed to shed the water.

Since we'd been traveling more or less behind the wagon company the whole time we'd been with them, most of the dead were still strangers. It's not usual in the west to be strangers, but we were. Mr. Jackman had taken delight in sporting with the Brisks over their ox team . . . and over my presence, so the other members of the company had held back their friendship, not wanting to be on Jackman's bad list. We knew the members of the company's names, but knew nothing about them so we couldn't send notice of their death to any of their relatives.

A fine breaker plow lay near a smoldering wagon. It's heavy hardwood beam burned nearly off, the share, colter, moldboard, and landslide made it one of the fanciest plows I'd ever seen. It had apparently been tied to the side of a wagon with thongs. When the thongs burned, the plow fell to the prairie grass. Seldom were whole plows transported by pioneers anyway . . . just the metal parts were transported, to save space.

The prairie itself had caught fire, burning a black circle for nearly a quarter mile, but as the grass was still green the fire never really got going good.

The Indians had taken the food and most of the clothes, leaving most of the wagons empty. In other wagons I found blackened coins and even a sack of partly melted gold dust. I carefully scooped up the gold dust and put it in my saddle bag. It was about five pounds worth.

Picking up the plow and resting it on the pommel, I swung into the saddle. Then, cuddling the plow like a baby, I picked my way back to the Brisks' wagon. Overhead the buzzards circled, waiting to reclaim their feeding grounds.

As I rode up, Julienne, Mae, and Hector stared at me anxiously. "They're all dead or taken captive," I said, as I handed down the plow to Julienne and Mae. "I was able to salvage this plow, which you'll need when you get to Oregon. In my saddle bag is about five pounds of partly melted gold dust."

"Was it Indians?" Julienne asked. It surprised me that she should ask, but then I realized that she had been set upon by white folks not many weeks earlier and feared some whites as much as Indians.

"Yes, it was Indians," I said. "The men killed were stripped and scalped. Most of the women and children were taken captive as I didn't see many of their bodies."

"What do Indians do with their captives?" Mae asked.

"They usually adopt the children, and the women become slaves and eventually wives. It's not an easy life, but no life is easy."

"They say you were a slave when Brigham Harold rescued you," Mae said.

"Yes, I was a slave once," I said, and left it at that.

"Should . . . should we bury the dead?" Julienne timidly asked.

"No," I replied. "We don't want to leave any evidence of our passing. Nature has it's own way of taking care of the dead."

That's heathen!" Mae accused. "Civilized people always bury the dead. If you don't, the wolves and buzzards will get at their bodies."

"It's not heathen! It's Earth Mother's own way of cleansing herself."

"It's heathen!" Mae insisted, stamping her foot for emphasis. "If'n you were really a Christian, you'd know that!"

I looked to Julienne, but she was studying the ground, not wanting to meet my gaze. I sensed that she, too, had strong feelings about leaving the dead unburied. She just wasn't so outspoken as Mae.

"All right!" I said, knowing I was defeated. "I'll bury 'em. But I'll do it myself . . . alone. When it gets dark I'll slip back and bury 'em."

Under cover of darkness I made my way to the massacre sight. I had good reason for not taking any of the Brisks along: I didn't want them to see the mutilated bodies 'cause they judge Indians far too harshly as it is. I don't understand why Indians mutilate bodies, either. Some say it is so they can't wander around as ghosts, looking for their scalps. Mainly, though, it's just like white soldiers who might spit on the bodies of fallen enemies, then kick them so's to make sure they're really dead.

I didn't expect to meet any Indians, but I was careful in my approach anyway. Peering up over the edge of the gully, the same gully the Indians had hidden in for their ambush, I saw it was safe. One at a time I dragged the bodies to the gully to make one mass grave. Then I caved dirt in a-top them, but I still had to do some shoveling. Next, I erected a Christian cross. Mormons don't put much stock in crosses, but guessin' that none of the dead were Mormons I thought they might appreciate it. Last, I quoted some scriptures from Alma about the resurrection of the dead. The dead may not have been Mormon, but those scriptures should make anybody feel better about dyin'.

As I rode back to camp, a night wind came up. It was as if Thunder Bird was on the side of Mae and Julienne, trying to hide tracks.

We were alone, just one wagon alone on the prairie. It was something the Brisks had experienced before, 'cept this time I was with them. They looked to me for leadership; but what could I do? I was just an Indian boy, though some say I had above average skills in weaponry.

Yet I'm a man given to fasting and prayer, as the white folks call it. Indians call it communication with the Great Spirit, or Manitou. Being responsible for the Brisks worried me and I felt a need to pray. I hid the Brisks in a grove of trees on a creek and went in search of a secluded spot.

I sang the chants of my heritage and prayed the prayers of the white man. When the cool of the evening set in I didn't build a fire since I didn't know the location of my enemies. Instead I wrapped myself in a buffalo robe and continued my prayers and chants.

Sometime during the night, I slept, and while I slept, I dreamed. In my dreams I saw myself preparing the Brisks' wagon to slink through the prairie in the darkness of the night. Overhead I saw Hercules in his place in the heavens, watching our flight. Then I saw myself crossing rivers and fighting enemies, helping the Brisks along. But I was not alone. By my side from the Spirit World was a man dressed as a Shoshone warrior. He was my father.

When my dream was over I awoke and lay there thinking. I was puzzled as to why my father should take such an interest in the Brisks. Were our lives to be somehow bound together?

It was gray in the east when I returned to the Brisks' wagon. I started threading strips of rawhide and gunny sack through the loops of the chains and everything that jingled. Hector brought in the oxen to be yoked, but I stayed him.

"We'll not be moving out 'til the moon comes up," I said. He was confused, so I explained.

"We'll travel by night 'til we reach the South Fork of the Platte. As we travel, we won't talk. Instead we'll communicate with the call of a quail and the yip of a fox." Hector didn't fully understand, but he seemed excited about it.

Julienne and Mae cooked cornbread and hard tack, which we would eat as we traveled. They also roasted an antelope that I had run down, afoot. Mae and Hector were amused at my running down the antelope, but I explained to them that every older Shoshone boy can do it, as can some of my Mormon friends at Manti.

A young Shoshone boy catches butterflies and rubs the wings on his chest to borrow their agility and speed. Then he practices running until he gets fast. By the time he's an older boy he starts running down antelope. Antelope have lots of speed but not much endurance. And since they drop from exhaustion, there's not too great a danger of an antelope turning on you. Still, you have to be careful.

Well, I ran down the antelope and we cooked it all, slicing the meat to eat in days to come. White folks are not big on eating antelope 'cause they think it's too strong, but they'll eat it if they are hungry enough. Course, even Indians would rather eat buffalo than antelope.

While we waited for the cloak of darkness to cover the prairie I taught my little band the call of the quail and the yip of the fox. They did reasonably well for whites.

An early moon, full and bright, was up nearly as soon as the sun went down. The real quails called and the real foxes yammered. It was time to yoke our team.

Night travel is more for the white man than the Indian 'cause Indians believe there are sometimes unfriendly spirits in the night. Then, too, Indians don't navigate by the stars, as do whites. Indians usually stay within their territory and memorize landmarks . . . the north side of a tree or rock feels different from the south side, so you always know where the sunrise and sunset is without using stars. Indians don't refer to north or south, they refer to sunrise, sunset, and sunwise. Sunwise is clockwise. However, Pa— Brigham Harold—taught me to navigate by the stars, too. Knowing how to travel by the stars opens up a whole new world to a person with wanderlust, like myself.

Not totally silent, but silent enough, we moved out. The sky was studded with a million stars. They would give us enough light when the moon set. I rode ahead of the team by a hundred yards or more, my eyes roaming the prairie. I also watched my Appaloosa's ears, knowing her hearing was more sensitive than my own.

Behind me the oxen plodded. Though not nocturnal animals, they have good night vision and a natural reluctance to place their hooves in black holes. The sound of the rolling wagon wheels crunching over the grass and an occasional sound of an ox hoof was all the noise we made.

The first night's travel was uneventful, but on the second night, shortly after the moon set, my horse heard something. Her ears came up and I slipped the thong off my six shooter. She looked straight ahead, to the north, straight into a northern breeze. Quickly I gave the alarm, three quail calls. The rolling wheels behind me stopped, and for a time I listened. I tested the air and detected no campfire smell, though I thought I caught the smell of horses. After a while I slipped the thong back on my six shooter and ground hitched my horse. Then, bow in hand, I slipped through the night.

I found the camp easily and soon discovered it was the camp of the horse thieves, Harry and Mel.

I'm not a pleasant enemy, so if left to my Indian instincts I'd have simply slipped in and slit the horse thieves' throats. But I'm Christian now. I mean no disrespect, but Christianity, with it's forgive this and forgive that, can complicate things. Why wait for a trial when you know someone is guilty? Of course I know the answer. It all comes back to following established rules or making your own rules. Making your own soon leads to chaos, so Papa Harold says.

I let the horse thieves be and returned to the Brisks' wagon. Then silently we retraced our steps to a depression a mile back, 'cause I didn't want to get in front of Harry and Mel and run the risk of them seeing our wagon tracks. Our plan was to hold back and give the thieves time to move out of our way. Horseback, as they were, they could move out a lot faster than we could.

Come morning, the thieves pulled out, setting a northwesterly course. We spent the day where we were and come night we set a northeasterly course.

"I think this will be our last night of night travel," I announced as we started the team. "There's likely a river ahead, and it's probably the South Fork of the Platte."

"How do you know there's a river that close?" Mae asked.

"I don't know for sure, Mae, but it's a good guess. There are very few animal tracks around the water holes. That means there is plenty of water close. Also, the buffalo grass has been cropped off shorter than it was a few miles south. That could mean a large herd had been feeding. They would be more likely to feed leisurely if they were close to water."

When day dawned we had not reached the river, but we were close, so we traveled on. By mid-morning there it was, flowing lazily in front of us.

There were fewer trees on the South Platte than I had expected. But there were some and when we found them we found something we hadn't expected—a Cheyenne village.

It wasn't a permanent village. Fact is, I don't know that Cheyennes have permanent villages. It appeared to have about two dozen tepees. The wagon was a hundred yards behind me, but I expected some hunting party to spot us any minute since we didn't have any cover.

To the Indian's thinking, a stranger is an enemy. I explained that to the Brisks, and they were concerned.

"Do you suppose we can retrace our route before they see us?" Julienne asked.

"Not likely," I replied, "though it's a possibility. But I think we'll be safer if we drive right in and introduce ourselves. It's hard to hide in the prairie and nobody's afraid of a lone wagon. They could take us anytime they wanted."

"That's likely true," Julienne replied, "but is it safe to drive right in?"

"The safest thing to do is to become known and be no longer strangers." She looked worried but nodded in agreement.

• CHAPTER NINE •

Mae

Maybe I give Billy more credit than he deserves, but it seems he has all the right answers. I'm starting to have warm feelings towards him . . . I can't deny it. But they don't run very deep. How could they? A decent white girl just doesn't fall in love with an Indian . . . it just wouldn't be proper.

Still, Mama likes Billy too, and so does Hector. Perhaps we've just been on the prairie too long and lost our proper senses. But God knows we were relying on Billy, and under the circumstances it sure seemed proper to do so.

In civilized white settlements men don't go around without shirts, but this was Indian country. Billy slipped into the wagon and came out wearing a breech cloth and leggings. He was all Indian now. He stripped the saddle off his horse and threw it in the wagon. Riding his horse bareback, he looked like a real Indian warrior. I was glad he was on our side.

Long before we reached the village we were monitored by Cheyenne braves, yet no moves were made or words spoken. The hair on the back of my neck stood on end. I'd always been told that Indians are a mysterious people, wild and ferocious, and only half human. But Billy is Indian, yet most definitely human too.

We kept our two milk cows and our buckskin colt tied close. Mama, Hector, and I walked so close to the wagon that we almost got caught in the turning spokes of the wheels. Billy rode ahead, straight and tall, muscles rippling in the morning sun. On his back rested his bow and quiver of arrows and at his belt hung a patch of light brown hair. What was it?

A scalp!

I shuddered with the realization . . . the horse thief's scalp! As all Indians love to tell war stories, Billy had told us about the thieves sneaking into his camp and having to kill the one; but I hadn't realized he'd kept the scalp. But why should I be surprised—I already knew he was a savage.

Billy was Indian all right . . . all Indian when he wanted to be. Yet he saved the lives of white women and children on the prairie and could quote scripture. Did anybody, Indian or white, really know him?

A half mile outside the village, on the banks of the South Platte, Billy wheeled his mount and rode back to the wagon. "This is a nice grassy spot. You and Hector will set up camp," he said to Mama. "I'll take Mae with me to the village."

"But why take Mae to the village with you?" Mama asked, worried.

"First impressions are important, and it looks peaceful for a brave to ride into a strange village with his squaw."

I'm ashamed to say that the thought of sitting close to Billy on his horse excited me. But then I looked at the scalp hanging from his belt and remembered the differences between us.

"I won't do it," I said. "I'm *no* Indian's *squaw*." Now Mama was worried about me going into the village, but she hadn't liked the way I had spoken to Billy. I could see it in her eyes. It was that same look she had when she had cause to paddle me when I was little. Still, she held her tongue.

"Is it *really* necessary?" she asked Billy.

"Unless they see you as my property, you will still be strangers when I meet them . . . and I figure you'll be a lot better off as my slave than theirs.

"Less'n you think he's wrong, you'd better go," Mama said. It was clear *she* didn't think he was wrong. I didn't think he was wrong either, but I didn't like being called a squaw. Ma was starin' at me real hard, but I looked over her shoulder and saw Billy smile at my predicament.

"Mama, Billy's a sav—"

"You'll GO!" Mama yelled. "If'n you don't you'll find the Indians'll treat you a lot better'n I do."

I sat there with my mouth open and my face turnin' real red. Mama hadn't spoken to me that way since I was just a kid. I could see I had no choice but to become a squaw. Oh my, I was mad. Shutting my mouth I jumped down and stomped over to Billy's horse. As there were no stirrups Billy held down his hand to help me up. I slapped it away and tried to jump up on my own. I almost made it too, but horses' backs are slippery and I found myself looking up at the horse's belly.

"What are you doing Mae?" Mama asked, looking down at me from the wagon.

I didn't see that as a fit question to answer. I got back up and this time took Billy's hand. He easily pulled me up behind him. Digging in his heels, the horse started with a jump and I had to grab Billy tight to stay on. I just knew he did that on purpose. As mad as I was though, I couldn't help feeling the warmth of his skin and the tightness of his muscles. That excitin' feeling I had when I first thought of riding with him came back and when his horse slowed to a walk I didn't loosen my grip.

When we reached the village, Billy slowed to a walk. Villagers gathered around, dogs barked, and naked children gawked, but they made way. Billy said Indian children go naked until about age seven; not that they don't have clothes but the children prefer not to wear their clothes.

According to Billy, white folks consider Indian children spoiled 'cause Indian parents give their children very few restraints and don't spank 'em. It's especially annoying to captives, who get the brunt of the children's mischievousness. I wondered if he was speaking from experience, since he had once been a Ute captive.

Most of the tepees faced east, their flaps thrown open to the morning sun. There was surprisingly little litter around. In front of a tepee, Billy pulled rein. It was the chief's tepee, but how Billy knew it, I surely don't know. According to Billy most villages have two chiefs, a camp chief and a war chief. I suspected this was the camp chief's tepee.

"Swing down, Mae," Billy said. I did. He followed and handed me the reins.

"Stand by the Appaloosa's head," he said, "and hold the reins firmly. The horse might get spooked, so be prepared. But stand straight and tall; look straight forward and be proud!"

Some of the braves were ogling me, and it made me nervous. But I stood my ground, looking proud, like Billy said. Billy was speaking to an older Indian who I took for the chief. He spoke a mixture of Indian and sign language, so I didn't know what was said.

After a while Billy and the chief sat cross legged on the ground and continued their conversation. Then, from his belt, Billy extracted a knife, and with two hands, presented it to the chief. Present giving, I remembered, was a part of Indian protocol.

For thirty minutes to an hour they talked, and I was growing weary. Still I did my part, standing straight and tall, holding the Appaloosa's reins. The horse stood three legged, almost going to sleep on her feet, as horses do. Finally Billy arose, face expressionless, and walked to me. Taking the reins he swung onto the horse's back and helped me up behind him.

"What did he say?" I asked, as we cantered to our camp.

"He said he would give two horses for you."

"He what?"

"He said you were a fine woman and well trained . . . he wanted to buy you for two horses."

"Two horses!" I replied.

"That's what I told him, only I didn't put it that way. I told him that you gave me great pleasure and were worth ten, maybe fifteen horses."

I doubled up my fists and hit him, but it didn't seem to make any impression at all, 'cept to make him laugh. It was good to hear him laugh.

When we got back to our camp, he held my hand as I slid to the ground. It seemed that he held it a little longer than necessary, but I was reluctant to pull it away.

Three days we camped near the Cheyenne village but after the first day, I saw Billy only once. That once was when he stopped by with a Cheyenne hunting party and left a young antelope. Mama tried to speak to him about future plans, but he shrugged it off, saying there was a more pressing matter that needed his attention. What could be more pressing than getting on with our journey? After all, the wagon trains along the Oregon Trail weren't a-going to wait for us. But we could do nothing without Billy, so we waited.

During those days my thoughts often turned to Billy . . . how it sounded to hear him laugh and how it felt to ride behind him, my arms around his chest. Then my thoughts would turn to the brown scalp at his waist. I was more than a little confused.

Mid-afternoon of the fourth day, Billy rode into camp "hell-bent-for-leather," as Papa would say. "Hide the team and wagon," he yelled, "and the colt and milk cows, too! The Cheyenne village is about to be attacked!"

You never seen us move so fast! We whipped the canvas and wagon bows from the wagon quicker than scat to give the wagon a lower profile. Then, in a tight little grove, we hid the wagon and tied the animals securely.

"Follow me!" Billy yelled. He led us along the river, but a girl wearing a skirt can't keep up with a boy, especially an Indian. I was running as fast as I could when I tripped and went down hard. The fall nearly knocked the wind out of me but it gave Mama and Hector time to catch up. I noticed that Billy didn't come back to help me. I guess war was no place for the gentlemanly arts. But still I wished he would have come back.

Halfway to the village, Billy turned abruptly and splashed across the river. We followed. Then he led us into a dense thicket at the base of a bluff. There, in a large washed out place in the bank, the Cheyenne women and children were gathered. They made room for us.

I figured this was a fight between Indians who had been fighting each other for years, and I didn't want to get caught up in their scrabble. But I knew that sure as shooting, with us camped by them, we would be considered fair game.

"Stay here," Billy ordered, and started to leave.

I watched him go, feeling a deep hole growing inside me. We would be safe here, but what about Billy?

Suddenly I realized that Billy was going, really going. He might die and I would never see him again. As I watched him splash through the river, all my pent up aversion to Indians seemed to amount to nothing.

When Billy found us out on the prairie, we were as good as dead. He brought us safety, and he brought us his child-like faith in the Great Spirit as he called upon God. I'd even started praying again. We'd lost Papa. We'd lost the farm in Texas. We'd lost our friends in the wagon train in Texas. We . . . I . . . must not loose Billy!

"I can help! I can load guns!" I called to Billy.

Billy stopped and turned around. "No!" he replied. "Only the men fight!" He turned and started back across the river.

Suddenly I made up my mind. "Bye, Mama," I whispered. "I'm going to load ammunition."

I'm sure Mama said something, but I didn't hear it. I was splashing across the river after Billy.

Halfway up the bank on the far side of the river Billy heard me splashing after him and turned. His angry eyes held mine for a moment; then he glanced across the river to where Indian women were sprinkling dirt and leaves over our tracks.

"I told you I could load guns!" I said. Then more gently I added, "I can load as fast as any boy."

Maybe his eyes softened a little . . . I don't know. He cast a second glance across the river, wondering. The Indian women had completed their camouflage task.

"Come!" he snapped. "It's too late to send you back."

Billy led to a spot on the top of a small bluff on the south side of the river. Water had formed a run-off, which had filled with new grass. It was a good spot since the casual observer wouldn't suspect it was there.

I watched the Cheyennes slip through the grass, taking up their positions. There was something graceful about the way they moved. They seemed to be appendages of the earth, the grass, the wind. They didn't fight the land, but lived with it. They lived so . . . easily . . . peacefully here in their little camp out in the middle of nowhere. They made us whites seem awkward and cowardly as we bounced across the prairie in our wagons and fearfully circled them each night. While the whites sat around the fire at night worrying about the weather, sickness, the food supply, the Indians lived simply, in tune with . . . the Great Spirit.

For a moment I felt proud there beside Billy—Walking Short—a full-blooded Shoshone. Somehow I felt that Papa wouldn't disapprove. Oh, he would disapprove of me being there in the battle—but not of me being next to Billy.

It occurred to me that Billy had been assigned this position by the war chief. Possibly he had secured a reputation as a marksman on the hunting trips of the past three days. Indians are poor marksmen with a rifle. Billy told me that's because they haven't developed the art of making bullets. If you don't have bullets to practice with it's hard to become a good marksman.

From our position we could see women in the village, calmly going about their usual activities. An old man was straightening an arrow with a sharp rock.

The village wasn't empty!

"There are still people in the village," I whispered to Billy. "Shouldn't they take refuge before the enemy comes?"

"Would you attack an empty village?" he replied.

"Well . . . no, I guess I wouldn't."

"In the village are the old ones. They are the decoys."

"That's cruel!" I whispered.

Billy hesitated, then calmly replied, "Every man earns his keep. When you get old you do what you can. The elderly are doing their part and trusting us to do ours."

I'd heard blow-by-blow descriptions of Indian attacks, but all the attacks I'd ever heard of were hit and run, slip-in-and-slip-out attacks. Yet the way we were positioned, it appeared as if the Indians expected the enemy to come riding in big as life, just a-waitin' to be shot down. I didn't understand what was going on, but I kept my peace.

Quiet settled over the village. Gradually the insects started to make their usual sounds and the birds began to chirp. All of a sudden Billy gave a bird chirp, which sounded like the other birds I'd been hearing. Only then did I realize I wasn't listening to real birds but to Indian signals.

It was so peaceful I had to remind myself that we were under attack. There I lay, just a-thinking, wondering what I was doing. It's strange where fate leads us. To my side was Billy . . . an Indian, but my friend. Instead of holding hands, we were holding rifles. All around me, though I couldn't see them, were men of a race I had loathed, and yet here we were on the same side. The Indians had given us refuge, and now we had to fight for them—with them.

As I watched Billy, he relaxed. But as he relaxed, I grew tense, 'cause I was beginning to read him. When the going gets tough, he's his calmest.

He sighted down his rifle barrel, and took up the trigger slack. I peeked out and almost screamed at what I saw.

White men!

It was white men attacking the Cheyenne village! Thinking they had caught us by surprise they were crawling on their stomachs toward the camp. We would be killing white men! It was too much for my brain to handle and I just quit thinking.

All of a sudden the air was pierced with a Cheyenne war cry so horrible it struck terror into my heart. Then Billy began firing.

"Gun," he said, handing me back his empty rifle. I couldn't move. "Gun!" he yelled. I handed it to him and began loading his empty one. My fingers didn't work right at first and I dropped shells into the grass. Billy had to wait a few seconds before I had the reloaded gun ready for him but he said nothing. I got better and soon was ready whenever Billy's rifle was empty. I didn't think, but just put myself on automatic. I heard more horrible war cries, I heard men screaming, and smoke stung my eyes. But none of it got to me 'cause I was a-loadin' rifles. Billy handed me an empty rifle, took up a loaded one, and I continued loading. The process repeated itself again and again.

The thunder of hooves was loud in my ears, and I glanced up to see a roan horse bearing down upon us. We were goners, I was certain. But I wasn't afraid—I wasn't anything. A moment before the horse was to trample us it jumped clean over us as if we were a ditch, or a fence. On the horse was a man wearing a Confederate Army shirt. That was the side my papa gave his life for. I saw an arrow pierce the man's back, followed by a second. Then the man fell, but he was drug by one foot which was caught in his stirrup.

I didn't know the battle was over until Billy didn't grab the loaded gun I held for him. My ears were ringing from the gun shots, but suddenly everything was quiet. Numbly I leaned forward and looked over the bank. What I saw horrified me. Indians were hurrying among the dead stripping them, taking scalps, and cutting the bodies open with their knives.

"Wait here," Billy ordered, drawing his own knife. He leaped over the bank and I turned and vomited, and then vomited again, and again, until there was nothing left in my stomach. My head was whirling. I didn't understand what was going on. I pulled my knees up and buried my face in my dress. I hugged my legs hard but couldn't stop shaking.

I didn't hear Billy return until he called.

"Mae," he said.

I looked up and saw him standing there holding his knife in one hand and a bag made out of his legging in the other. It was full of something.

I was a mess inside, but when I spoke the words came out calm. "Savage," I said.

"Mae," Billy said again. He took a step toward me. Using my hands and my feet I scooted backwards.

"Stay away from me, you butcher!" I said, and I meant it. I grabbed the loaded gun Billy had left with me and held it on him. At that moment I had it in me to shoot Billy, and he knew it; but still he was as calm as a summer day.

"What do you mean butcher?" he asked. "I didn't kill anybody that wasn't a'goin' to kill us first."

"Killin' them white men was one thing," I hissed. "But butchering them after they was dead is another!"

Billy stood for a long minute without saying a thing. He just looked me deep in the eyes. He wasn't angry, he wasn't afraid—it was like he was listening to the way I felt through his eyes. Finally he spoke. "Mae, I know what those Indians are doing seems savage to you, but what the white men would have done to the women would have been even more savage. What the Cheyenne are doing to the bodies doesn't bother me like it does you, but believe me Mae, I didn't touch one body with my knife. Here, look." He tossed the knife in the grass beside me. I glanced at it and the blade was shiny clean.

"You could'a cleaned it," I said. My voice was beginning to shake. "Besides, what's in the bag?"

He tossed it at my feet and out of it fell books and papers. I saw a Bible and some envelopes that looked like letters. I stared at the contents so hard that Billy could have safely disarmed me, but he didn't move. "I just took what the Cheyenne didn't want, this bein' their victory and all. From those letters I thought I could write to some of their kin and tell them they had died."

It couldn't be true. Even I wouldn't have though of doing that. "I don't believe you!" I said. "Killing and mutilating white men . . . You're a savage!" Now I was yelling.

"Go ahead and pull the trigger, Mae," he said quietly.

"What?"

"I said if you really believe that, pull the trigger. I'd just as soon be dead as have you really believe I'm a savage."

"Then I'll do it," I said, bringing the barrel to aim at his chest. "I'll do it!" But I didn't do anything. Billy stepped up to me and gently took the rifle away. He sat down beside me and took me in his arms. I didn't stop him, but I didn't respond either. With one hand he turned my head so that I had to look into his eyes. There was no savageness in them, just hurt from what I had said, hurt for what I had seen.

Then I started bawling like I had never bawled before. I must have shown no sign of stopping 'cause Billy picked me up and carried me like a baby back to the wagon where Mama and Hector were anxiously waiting for us. He handed me to Mama and I cried myself to sleep in her arms.

• CHAPTER TEN •

Mae

I woke late the next morning, but Mama and Hector were still asleep. The excitement of the battle the day before took a lot out of us. I walked stiffly down to the river and took a long drink and splashed water on my face. I still felt shaky. But the bright sunshine and the tall grass dancing a graceful dance in the gentle breeze calmed my nerves. Yesterday seemed to have been a dream—an almighty bad one. I was still kneeling by the creek when I heard what sounded like an Indian chant floating on the breeze. It was coming from the opposite direction of the village so I figured it must be Billy.

I had been just plain mean to Billy after the battle, but I can't say that I was in my right mind. Still the things I had said were unforgivable. I felt shame as I remembered how gently Billy had carried me back to camp even after the things I said to him. I figure I didn't deserve such kind treatment.

I got up and walked along the river into the wind. The chant got louder and finally I spotted Billy sitting Indian style on a grassy bank under some cottonwoods. I don't understand Indian prayer and didn't know whether it was wrong for another person to join in, but Billy looked peaceful and his chant sent warm tingles through my body.

Walking up quietly, I took a seat facing Billy. With his eyes he acknowledged me and then stared over my shoulder

across the river as he continued the chant. Closing my eyes
I let the chant lift my body and carry it along just above the
grass. I felt as though I were one with the eagles, with the
grasses, with the wind—with all of nature. I didn't know
what Billy was saying, but I felt a peace, a joy, fill my soul.
The chant stopped and I opened my eyes to meet Billy's—
dark and gentle.

"We usually pray with our eyes open so that we can see
the work of the Great Spirit as we commune," Billy said.

"But I did see," I answered.

"That is good."

"I have some things to say to you, Billy, if'n I can say
them."

"You don't need to say anything," he responded, calmly.

"Oh, but I do. I'm sorry about . . . I shouldn't ha . . .," I
had thought I was all cried out, but more tears were wet-
ting my cheeks. "The words all seem wrong."

"Why don't you tell the Great Spirit—God—then. No
matter what words you use, if you are sincere, he under-
stands."

I hadn't prayed out loud since we had first been abandoned in the prairie and wondered if God would listen to
me. "Would you pray with me?" I asked. "Then I think God
would be more likely to listen."

I was surprised to see Billy get immediately to his
knees. I followed suit and, in a hesitant voice, I said, "Dear
God, you heard what I said last night and you know it
wasn't nice. But I just don't understand what I saw. You
know I'm sorry for what I said, sorrier than I've ever been
in my life. Please tell Billy that and I hope you'll both forgive me. I sure miss Pa, God, and wish he were with us.
Please tell him we love him. Today's a new day. Please help
me to live and be happy. I . . . I love you God. In Jesus
name, amen."

I opened my eyes and wiped them dry. Billy stayed on
his knees and smiled at me.

"Okay?" I asked.

"Enough said," he answered.

We got up and walked side by side back to camp. I think God was already answerin' my prayers, 'cause I was feeling mighty happy.

"We'll be moving out in the morning," Billy announced over breakfast.

"Why did we have to wait so long to get on our way?" Mama asked. "We've been here four days."

I knew the answer, but only because Billy had told me. "It wasn't safe to move until now," he said.

"I don't understand. Do you think the horse thieves are still around?"

"The horse thieves weren't the threat, the Cheyenne were. There are only two horse thieves, but there are many Cheyenne, and they love to count coup."

"The Cheyenne are friendly to us, never once givin' us a moments trouble."

"They were friendly because we were camped next to them. Most tribes won't bother strangers who come into their village, so we were safe. But we were safe only as long as we were there. Once we left we would be fair game for plunder, so we had to watch our chances to leave safely.

"It's different now," he continued, "because we fought beside them. In most of the Indian world, the meaning of brotherhood is to fight beside each other. If we hadn't fought beside them, we might have died beside them, as the deserters would have killed and plundered us right along with the Cheyenne. And I assure you, Mrs. Brisk, you and Mae would have been a much more rewarding treasure to the deserters than the Indian women, as you are of the deserter's race."

Mama shuddered, and so did I. It was something to consider. We owed our lives to Billy's Indian savvy. I touched his arm, then looked into his eyes. "Thank you," I whispered. For just a second I thought I saw him blush. Then I grinned, 'cause I didn't know Indians blushed.

Come first light we yoked the team and drove 'em across the river, setting a northerly course. The oxen seemed to have a new lilt to their steps. More 'n likely the four days of rest were something they needed.

Ahead of us was Pole Creek, flowing into the South Platte somewhere to the east. Still farther north was Smith Fork, flowing northeast into the North Platte. Then we'd travel along the Oregon Trail, which followed the south bank of the North Platte, and we'd pass Chimney Rock and Scott's Bluff. Then we'd reach Fort Laramie. At least that's the way Billy described our route, and he seemed to know.

People in the West seldom carried tally books with them—they memorized. With all their fancy learning, many people of education have never cultivated the art of memorization. For those who can't write, it's different. When you can't write you have to memorize and remember. Many a drifter can tell you in detail of places he's never been but only heard about around a campfire. Though he could read, Billy was that way, 'cause he's a good listener. With skill, Billy led us knowledgeably across a land where his feet had never trod.

"I'll leave you at Pole Creek," Billy announced the next day, "and do some hunting."

"But we have plenty of meat," Mama replied.

"We are closing in on the Oregon Trail, which is heavily traveled. Hunters have been fanning out on both sides of the trail harvesting game for thirty years and now the hunting there is poor. I saw signs of antelope back there a spell."

It all made sense, though we hoped he would kill buffalo rather than antelope. But whatever game he killed, we'd eat, and be thankful for it. At Pole Creek we made camp, and while Billy hunted we built a wickiup for smoking the meat.

Mid-afternoon, Billy returned, but we were disappointed, as there was no game behind his saddle. "I'll need the wagon," he explained. "I killed a couple of buffalo a mile west of here." Excitedly we unloaded our meager possessions from the wagon and yoked the oxen.

"You'd better take Mae to drive the oxen and help load the meat," Mama counseled. "Hector and I can start the smoking fires, and get the brine ready." So I drove the oxen, and Billy rode his Appaloosa. I would have liked him to ride beside me on the wagon seat, but that was not Billy's way. He preferred the freedom of a horse's back. He rode ahead looking for danger while I followed a hundred yards behind.

The buffalo, dead in the afternoon sun, were already being attacked by the buzzards. They protested our presence but flew away when we butted in. Billy had already gutted the animals, but together we butchered them, Shoshone style.

The way the Shoshones butcher a buffalo is different from anything you ever saw. They cut the animal along the back bone from head to tail and take off the top half of the hide. Then they cut away all the meat to the bone. After that they tie a rope to the feet and using a horse, pull the carcass over.

The hides on the big seven-foot prairie buffalo are mighty heavy. Half a hide is enough for the women, who usually butcher the animals. You can rip the hide off with the help of a horse, but sooner or later you have to scrape all the fat and flesh from the hide to tan it.

We placed the hides in the bottom of the wagon, raw side up, and loaded chunks of meat atop them. When I whipped up the team, it was a hard pull.

When we got back to camp, Mama and Hector were ready for us, so we set to work cutting the meat, washing it in the brine water, and hanging it up to dry or smoke. The brine water removes much of the blood and cures the meat. Smoking partly cooks the meat, making it tenderer than sun dried. It's not the Indian method of curing of meat, it's the white man's method. Indians just cut the meat in strips up to six feet long and let 'em dry in the sun.

Billy didn't help us cure the meat, a job which took several days. He's strictly a hunter. I've noticed that once the meat is in camp, he usually has nothing to do with it, which is the Indian way. He was out hunting again when the visitors came.

The visitors were white men. They weren't wicked, but they were mischievous.

Hector saw them first and came a-running. "Mama," he breathlessly announced. "There's a bunch of men on horses coming up the creek!"

"How many?" Mama asked, calmly. Her calmness belied her inner feelings, as Indians aren't the only people suspicious of strangers.

"There are four riders. Two of 'em are leading pack animals."

"Mae," Mama directed, "get the pistol and hide it in the folds of your skirt." She was speaking of the pistol Billy had taken from the horse thief, the thief he'd scalped.

"Won't be necessary," came a voice. We all turned to see a man step from behind the wagon. "And there aren't four o' us, there's five."

"Who are you?"

"Bat's the name, Bat Gibson, though I haven't had it long. I find it advantageous to change names from time to time."

"What do you want?"

"Isn't it obvious? We're five lonely men, but some corn pones, fried in buffalo grease will do for a start. If'n you got some sugar, you might cook up a mess of bear signs. I could smell that buffalo grease a mile down wind, and it made my mouth water."

"Don't have any sugar," Mama replied, her voice controlled, "But Mae and I will whip up some corn pones."

Mama already had the corn batter mixed and was dropping the first drops of dough in the hot grease when the four riders that Hector had seen, joined Gibson. The four swung down and made themselves at home. It was obvious they counted us as their prisoners and property.

"These gentlemen are my friends, ma'am," Gibson drawled. As relaxed as if he were at a Sunday social, he started introducing his fellow riders. "The ugly man there is Rex Allen, and next to him is Ohio McGovern, Martin Westlake, and the old codger is Thomas Cast." The introduction was highly unusual 'cause in the West it's the person that counts, not the names. But although they were introduced in the manner of gentlemen, they didn't act like gentlemen. They went snooping into our belongings, which were still stacked beside a tree where we'd put them when we unloaded the wagon to retrieve the buffalo meat.

"Where's your man?" Gibson asked.

"He's off hunting," Mama replied.

"You're lying," Cast put in. "There hain't no man's clothes among your belongings. I think you're a widow lady." Turning to Hector he asked, "Where's your pa, son?"

"Papa was killed at Shiloh," Hector answered. "He died fighting for the Confederacy."

"He surely was fighting on the wrong side," Ohio drawled. "But that's neither here nor there. When are them corn pones a-goin' ta be ready?"

"By the time you get your plates, they'll be ready," Mama replied. If there had been only one man, Mama might have rendered him helpless by splashing hot grease in his face as she was serving him. But with five men there was always someone watching. So Mama served 'em, and they sure could eat! They ate like Indians, eating as if they were putting a week's worth of eating into one meal. Mama was cooking her third batch of batter before they showed any signs of slowing down. Men who live off the land eat mostly meat and crave bread stuff.

We learned they were five drifters on their way to New Mexico, though it wasn't clear why they weren't using the Santa Fe Trail. They had trailed a cattle herd from Texas to Kansas, then gone on to St. Louis, came west from St. Louis along the Oregon Trail and were now crossing overland to New Mexico.

Finished eating, Westlake dug into his saddle bag for a mouth organ. To my horror, the men wanted to dance.

I like to dance, but not with the likes of these drifters. Menfolks should come to a dance freshly bathed and wearing a clean shirt. Their beards should be trimmed, and they should have cleaned their breath with mint leaves. But these men were right off the prairie and not fit companions for a social. Yet one of them grabbed Mama, and one me, and set us a-dancin'.

For hours we danced. Not that it was all that bad, but I wasn't in the mood. And we would have been dancing longer had not one o' them yelled, "The horses are loose!"

Sure enough the horses were wandering out on the prairie, trailing their halter ropes. The man named Cast stayed to guard us while the rest raced after their horses. What concerned the drifters was that the picket pins had been pulled—someone had started the horses a-drifting.

Mama and I sat down, thoroughly exhausted, glad for the reprieve. Yet our minds were calculating, considering how we could get the drop on Cast. We could hear the cursing of the drifters as they hiked to their mounts. A cowboy will dance for hours in his riding boots, yet if he has to walk farther than the corral, he grumbles.

"How did the picket pin get pulled?" I whispered to Hector.

"Don't know," he replied, "but I suspect Billy." I, too, suspected Billy.

Near the horses, suddenly an Indian appeared out of the grass and let out a Cheyenne war cry as he vaulted astride one of the mounts. He appeared to be dressed as a Cheyenne High Warrior, yet in my mind I thought only of Billy. Pistols seemed to materialize in the drifters hands, yet they couldn't shoot for fear of hitting their mounts. The Indian was laying on his mount's back, slightly to the side away from the drifters.

Oh the drifters were mad! Such cursing I never heard in all my born days. But that Indian, whoever he was, was cunning and made off with all seven animals.

Cast, too, was cursing, and stopped only when he heard the click . . . the click of Mama cocking the shotgun.

"My finger is starting to shake from all that dancing," Mama coldly said. "I'd relax some if'n you'd put your hands on your head."

"Do you want me to unbuckle my gun belt?" Cast asked.

"Of course not. If'n your hands so much as twitch from the top of your head, if you even think about twitching one of them, my finger will twitch on this here trigger."

Staying clear of Cast, I retrieved my own pistol from the wagon. Now there were two of us armed.

"Sit down!" Mama ordered and Cast sat, cross legged, his back to us.

The situation was delicate, and I wondered what Mama would do. Then I saw Hector forming a lariat from a tiny rope. He flipped the lariat once, twice, and on the third try he lassoed Cast's revolver butt as neatly as you please and drew the weapon to him. It was a new gun, the likes of which I'd never seen. It was a Smith and Wesson .44, new and shiny.

Angry and cursing, the four cowpokes trudged back to our camp. The trees largely hid our activities from them. When they entered the shade of the trees they were startled to be looking into the black holes of our guns. They were cautious too, though not especially worried. After all, they figured that given a little time they could get the upper hand on two women and a boy.

"Now see here, ma'am," Allen said, "There's no call for that." It was the first step of a technique to get Mama off guard, and both Mama and I knew it. They'd get her into a conversation, and sooner or later they'd find a weakness.

"You're five men, alone. No horses, no pack animals, and you're stranded on the prairie."

"What of it?"

"More 'n likely the next thing you'll do is steal my wagon and team, 'cause you've got no transportation of your own!"

"Look ma'am. We treated you well—"

"Treated us well!" Mama broke in. "You ate a week's worth of food and forced Mae and me to dance with you. Do you know what you smell like? You smell like buffaloes! How long has it been since you bathed?"

They looked at each other uneasy like. "Just last week I waded across the creek . . . got plumb wet clear to my waist!" Allen exclaimed.

"Hector?" Mama said. "Get a bar of lye soap. Mr. Allen is about to lead his companions into the creek for the bath of their lives!"

"Look here . . . ," Allen started to say.

"You think I'm joking?" Mama asked.

"N . . . n . . . no ma'am," Martin Westlake put in. "But we'll not bathe with you watching."

"March!" Mama yelled, ignoring his modesty. The men, all of 'em, started for the creek. I don't think the men were scared. They probably thought they could draw and shoot before Mama got off a shot. But there was no use taking a chance, and these weren't really bad men, they were just misguided. And you don't up and shoot a woman in the West for ordering you to take a bath. For one thing, white women in the West are scarce as hens' teeth, 'cept among the Mormons. Besides, the drifters knew they had a bath coming.

At the edge of the creek they stopped and timidly looked back at Mama. Mama was partly behind a tree, shotgun still ready for business.

"Well," Mama said, "are ya going to march into the creek with your guns on, or are you going to leave 'em on the dry bank?"

Gingerly they unbuckled. It was a tense moment. Any one of them could have seized the opportunity to draw his gun. But there was always the chance that Mama, if pushed, would pull the trigger, and a shotgun is a fearsome thing. So they bided their time, waiting for a better opportunity, and for the moment gave Mama her way. Gingerly they placed their gun belts on the dry shore.

In the water they waded, and only when they were waist deep did any of them start to strip off.

"Get back there and keep bathing!" Mama yelled to Ohio, when he started to return to shore. Truth is, she didn't know what to do with the men. She was hoping Billy would return to take charge, and was stalling for time.

"This has gone far enough," Ohio replied. "We need to get on with the tracking of our horses!"

"How much chance do you have of finding 'em?" Mama replied. They knew what Mama was getting at. Their horses were all but lost 'cause there is no way in God's green earth that they could catch a Cheyenne horse thief before he got the horses back to his band or village, they being afoot. Yes siree, that Cheyenne would be a big man in his village tonight!

Out of the corner of my eye I saw Billy slip into camp. He was dressed, not as an Indian, but as a white man and was wearing a pistol. It was the best sight I ever did see all day.

Billy spoke quietly to Hector, then stepped up beside Mama. Hector responded to Billy's whispered message by retrieving the drifter's weapons.

"Looks to me like the womenfolk have caught themselves some sinners and are baptizing 'em," Billy drawled, loud enough for all to hear.

"Who are you?" Allen asked, startled.

"Name's Billy. You might say that Hector and I are the menfolks of the family."

"You're an Injun!"

"Very good," Billy mocked. "You're not as dumb as you look." They didn't like it but kept their mouths shut. "If'n you want to come to shore and get dressed, I'll send the womenfolk for a stroll up the creek to give you some privacy."

"We'd like that," Cast responded, chagrinned at the unexpected turn of events.

So we went for a stroll, leaving our guests to the care of Billy.

As we strolled along, a bluejay watched, perched on a branch with his head cocked to the left. It had it's own opinion of life, and loudly shared that opinion with us.

Under the trees, last fall's leaves were thick and crunchy. I looked out to the prairie. A few miles away the grass was as high as an ox's belly. It was shorter here, giving way to wild sage.

Mama and I walked along, kicking the leaves, relieved that Billy was now in control. After a respectable period of time we returned to camp.

The drifters had changed into fresh clothes, and Thomas
Cast was even trimming his beard. Rex and Bat were hun-
kered down by the creek, washing their soiled clothes.
Taking a good, hard look at the drifters, I noted that several of 'em looked a tat handsome, in a rough way. As a
body they all had a sheepish look about them.

All the men were wearing their gun belts and side arms,
and I gave a wondering glance at Billy. "Figured they might
feel lucky," he explained. "Besides, in this country it's more
dangerous to have 'em unarmed than armed." It was the
way of the West.

"Howdy ma'am," one man tipped his hat. He was followed by a chorus of polite greetings from the other men.

"Though we've dined and danced," Mama said to one,
"I'm afraid I don't remember your name?"

"Martin ma'am. Martin Westlake."

"Well Martin, freshly bathed you smell less like a buffalo, but you could use a shave."

"I'll take care of that, Mrs. Brisk."

"You do that, Mr. Westlake. But once you've shaven, how
do you plan on earning your keep? Looks to me like you're
destitute."

Westlake looked to the others, then returned his gaze to
Mama. "I don't know, ma'am. We'll need horses."

"Maybe you need a tracker."

"We can track 'em easy enough," he said. "But the horses
are likely in an Arapaho or Cheyenne village by now, and
that's a whole new ball of pemmican, ma'am."

"You could trade for them," Billy suggested.

"We've got little to trade, 'cept our outfits. We just came
off a cattle drive and have Union script, which doesn't hold
up too much with Indians."

"Looks to me," I said thoughtfully, "that you're missing
the obvious. Billy is wily as a fox when it comes to creeping
up to most anything. Ten-to-one he could retrieve your animals."

All eyes turned to Billy, who grunted like an Indian.
"Could do," he said. "It would be risky. If'n I got 'em back,

they'd be my property, and you'd have to trade me out of 'em, which might not be easy."

The men expected nothing less. But then Billy gave a hard look at Cast and said, "Your mount will cost you that new pistol you're packing."

Cast cursed. "Do you know what that gun is? It's the newest thing out . . . only two of 'em in St. Louis. It's too good for an Injun . . . meaning no disrespect."

There was a long pause, and Cast grew uneasy. When Billy spoke, his voice was slow, cold, and calculated. "You ought to feel lucky that it was returned to you after Hector lassoed it. But your horse will cost you that pistol." Billy started to leave, then almost as an afterthought, again turned his gaze back to Thomas Cast.

"I'll tell you what I'll do, Mr. Cast. If you can outshoot me, after I retrieve your animals, you can have the gun back."

Cast grinned. "You got yourself a deal," he said.

"Mister," Gibson said, "You just lost yourself a fine weapon. The only man that ever outshot Thomas Cast was Brigham Harold, and you just aren't in his class."

"Don't count on it, Gibson. Brigham is my white father."

Well, that took the wind right out o' their sails. They all just gawked.

Come night, Billy slipped out of camp. He was gone all night and most of the next day . . . guess he wanted it to look good. Come late afternoon, he came riding in, driving the drifters' horses before him. The drifters were pleased, for they had not had not had much hope that Billy would retrieve.

"I half believe you *are* Brigham's boy," Cast said, pleased at the horses' recovery. "Heard he got himself a Ute boy. Course it won't do you no good, 'cause I'm a-going to outshoot you."

"Not a Ute boy, a Shoshone boy, Mr. Cast. Just quit talkin', and set up your shooting range."

"It's already set up, Billy. Bat here will throw a knot into the air, and we'll see who can hit it the most times before it hits the ground."

"Fair enough," Billy agreed. "You shoot first."

Bat tossed a knot into the air, and Cast blasted away, hitting the knot three times before it hit the ground, though he fired six rounds. Then it was Billy's turn.

Again Bat tossed a knot into the air, and I'll have to give him credit for tossing it equally as high. With the ease of a professional, Billy palmed his pistol, and fired four rounds, striking the knot all four times.

Cast, looking as innocent as he could, had been reloading his Smith & Wesson. But obviously shocked by Billy's performance, he gaped. When the reports died away his only comment was, "Why didn't you fire six rounds?"

"The last two are reserved for you, to keep you honest, seeing that you were in such an all fired hurry to have a loaded gun when mine was empty," Billy replied, leveling his pistol at Cast's belt buckle.

"You handled that the way Brigham would have," Cast grinned. "I guess you really are his son, though you can't blame a man for trying."

• CHAPTER ELEVEN •

Mae

The drifters rode south; we started north. Ma drove the wagon, and Hector and I walked.

At Pole Creek we'd painted the outside of our wagon with a mixture of buffalo blood and skim milk as Billy suggested. It keeps the buckboard from weathering too badly. In Texas we'd oiled our canvas from some oil seeps we found, so we had a good tight shelter.

I was walking along near the rear of the wagon, listening to the sound of the butter splashing in it's buttermilk when Billy rode up close. It thrilled me to have him so near.

"Get your pistol," he advised. "We've got company."

I didn't see anyone, but being atop his Appaloosa, Billy could naturally see farther than I could. I fetched my pistol from it's nook in the wagon and strapped the gunbelt under my skirt. There was a rip in my skirt through which I could retrieve the weapon, if necessary.

Mama reached back into the wagon and retrieved Papa's rifle and shotgun. She placed them both close at hand.

Our "company" was six Sioux Indians. They were fine looking men and impressively attired. They followed us a hundred yards off. On the rump of one of the horses was a keyhole shaped design, like Billy's. And on the right front leg was a hash mark, also like Billy's.

"Billy," I said. "I've been meaning to ask you what the markings on your pony represent."

"Well," he said, pointing to the keyhole shaped mark, "this one is a medicine mark. It means I have communication with the Great Spirit . . . I know herbs and can set bones. Course I got most of my knowledge from my white father."

I was impressed. But as he didn't say anymore about it, I continued.

"What are the hash marks for."

"They're coup marks, meaning I've counted coup. It's the Indian's way of bragging."

"I thought you kept scalps when you counted coup."

"Well, yes and no. Without his scalp an enemy wanders the earth as a ghost. You don't want to have a whole army of enemy ghosts around, so you release the ghosts with a ceremony and retire the scalps. Warriors like to take the scalps back to the field of battle and leave 'em on a buffalo chip for Earth Mother to reclaim."

"Good idea," I said . . . amused, but trying to keep my face stoic. Billy cast me a hard look, and I decided I'd said too much.

"Mae," he began. "You have to have the scalp to prove the enemy is dead. But once you've shown off your trophy you have little use for it."

It made sense.

Come noon, we stopped, and Mama whipped up some buttermilk cornbread batter and fried it in butter. While she worked she kept an eye on the Sioux, as we all did.

Billy rode out and greeted them, hand raised, palm outward. When he returned, the Sioux were with him. At our wagon they swung down and shared a meal with us. Though they didn't speak a word of English, Billy communicated easily with them using sign language and a few words of Shoshone.

In the Indian world you eat 'til you're distended or 'til the food's gone. The Indians looked bewildered when we only offered them one plate of food. They liked Mama's cornbread and would have liked more. There was kind of a sad look in their eyes when we put the Dutch oven away and moved out.

"What do they want?" Mama asked when we were once again on the move.

"Nothing," Billy responded, unconcerned. "Nothing but company. Course they're curious. All us Indians are curious."

All afternoon they flanked us, and come nightfall we could see their fires. For two more days they flanked us, but on the morning of the fourth they were nowhere to be seen.

The North Platte was not many miles away, and we were in good spirits. But when we woke one morning, one of our oxen was laying on it's side, belly extended.

"Bloated," Mama said.

"What could he bloat on?" I asked.

"Don't know. Check the other stock, Mae." I checked and found that the other animals looked peaked but okay.

"More 'n likely it was the weeds we camped by," Billy said. "We need to move the animals to good grass."

Billy and I yoked the healthy ox and our milk cows to the wagon while Mama retrieved a long butcher knife from the kitchen items. It was sharp as a razor 'cause that's the way Mama kept her knives. The ox was going to have to be stuck, or it would die for sure.

Hector and I held down the ox though we didn't need to; the ox wasn't up to offering resistance. Then Mama, carefully calculating the positions of the animals organs, plunged the knife into the ox's stomach.

Foul smelling gas belched out with a rush, accompanied by some greenish-yellow liquid and some partly digested weeds. The ox struggled at first, then closed his eyes and relaxed in a sigh of relief.

"Stay with the sick ox, Mae, while we move the other animals," Mama directed. "We'll not move 'em far, maybe a half mile, and then we'll be back for you."

So I stayed with the sick ox and watched the team and

wagon as they made their way to good grass. They stopped three quarters of a mile away and picketed the animals on the good grass. Then Billy returned, jogging in a tireless rhythm, typical of most Indians I'd seen.

"How's the ox doing?" he asked as he reached me.

"He seems peaceful," I replied.

"Uh-huh," Billy muttered, as he studied the animal. "But he won't be useful for pulling the wagon for several days, even if he lives."

Following Billy's directions, we set to work making a poultice for the ox's wound using herbs Billy had in his possibles bag. The ox barely stirred as Billy tied the poultice in place around its belly. For nearly an hour the ox was content to lie there. Suddenly the animal struggled to its feet and, staggering like it was drunk, made its way toward the other animals.

With Billy and I flanking, the ox moseyed along, taking frequent rests. By and by we reached the wagon where the sick ox again enjoyed the company of the other animals.

The miles grew long under our feet and the sun burned hot. Our travel speed had to be controlled by the weakest of our animals. We couldn't use the cows to pull the wagon, 'cause if we did they'd dry up, and we wanted milk. But our wagon was relatively light, so Billy and Mama rigged the yoke to place most of the load on the healthy ox, although both oxen pulled. We would travel sometimes fifteen minutes, sometimes hours, before the sick ox showed signs of giving out. Then we'd rest. Gradually our travel time increased.

Because we were moving so slowly Billy had time to hunt, and he killed another buffalo. He suspected it was the last buffalo meat we would harvest for some time since we were getting close to the Oregon Trail. We stopped and cured the meat in sagebrush smoke as best we could while our ox healed.

Our wagon was now so full of smoked and dried meat we hardly had room for ourselves. But we were thankful for the meat. Fact is, this was the best Hector and I had ever eaten, and Hector was even gaining weight.

The pillows of white clouds cast occasional shadows on the tufts of raw grass beneath our feet. Every once-in-awhile we came across a lone sagebrush which was sheltering rodent holes or shading a sleeping rattler. The land was sloping, and in the distance a ribbon of greenery could be seen giving us cause to suspect we were nearing the North Platte. It was a ribbon of green grass, willows, and brushes, but there were no trees.

Following the Platte on the near side was the Oregon trail. It wasn't a single set of wheel ruts, but a wide trail; wide enough for wagons to travel six abreast. The trail was sometimes close, sometimes miles from the greenery and the water. Travelers don't like to camp too close to the water's edge, as it's easier to carry water than to battle insects. Still, good grass for the animals is the most important consideration.

We camped on the Oregon Trail and rejoiced, for it seemed like our troubles were at an end. The sick ox was on the mend, and in our minds we envisioned a wagon train bringing families and new friends. Life was good.

For two days we waited but saw no wagon trains. During this time our sick ox gained most of its strength back, so the morning of the third day we yoked our team and started West along the Oregon trail. Our travel was slow. We lacked reason to hurry and had faith a train would soon overtake us.

The hot July sun beat down on the vast prairie from a large cloudless sky. We saw hundreds of snakes, lizards, and sometimes whole clouds of grasshoppers. Our travel was through bunch grass and wild sage—ancient, gnarled. The soil was often sandy. In spots where there was no sand, it was powdery. The movement of our wagon and animals sent clouds of dust into the sky.

The night of our second day's travel we camped among trees. It was a spot where many travelers had camped, since there was good grass and water for the animals and trees that offered shelter. We unyoked the team and Billy unsaddled his mare. We watched as she rolled contentedly then took to cropping the grass like she was home.

We'd finished our evening meal, and there wasn't more than a few minutes of twilight left, when suddenly Billy grabbed his weapons and drifted into the shadows. He hadn't said a word, so we wondered . . . wondered and waited. But we didn't wait unprepared, no siree. Mama took up her shotgun, and I had my pistol in the folds of my skirt. It was full dark when the frail voice hailed us out of the night.

"Hello the camp?" It sounded like a child—a female child.

"Who are you?" Mama replied, shotgun in hand. She was partly concealed behind the wagon. I was on my belly under the wagon, Hector by my side.

"Minerva Tally, and I'm alone."

"Come on in, Minerva, but walk slowly. This here shotgun might go off if you aren't who you say you are."

She came out of the darkness, and Mama threw some brush on the fire to see by. There she stood, a skinny girl of about thirteen years in loose fitting clothes. Maybe she'd missed too many meals, I don't know. More often than not, you see children wearing too small o' clothes rather than too large.

"I'm camped the other side of the trees," she said. "I saw your campfire."

"You all alone?"

"I am. Papa died . . . buried him yesterday. I buried him deep, too, so the wolves wouldn't get him."

"Smallpox?" Mama asked.

"No, it was blood poisoning. Papa crushed his foot a month ago and it kept getting worse. A week ago the wagon master told us to stay behind and join the next train 'cause we were slowing the others down."

"How far behind you is the next train?"

"Don't know, and the wagon master didn't know either. But across the river I saw a Mormon company. The wagon master suggested I could join them, but I don't know about that. Folks say the Mormons are peculiar with strange ways. They say Mormons are Indian lovers."

"Could be," Mama replied. "I've known several of 'em, and I'd surely call 'em Indian lovers." There was a twinkle in her eye.

"Are you alone too?" Minerva asked. "I don't see any menfolks."

"We're alone, 'cept for Billy, who slipped out when he heard you approaching," Mama said and she put away her shotgun.

Minerva looked suspicious. "I walked almighty quietly."

"Could have," Mama replied, "But no matter how quietly you walk, the insects know you're around. Even I noticed the absence of crickets chirping when you approached."

Minerva seemed impressed at Mama's savvy. Then she glanced longingly at the cold remains of a buffalo roast.

"Are you hungry?" Mama asked.

"Yes. But don't get me wrong. I've got plenty of supplies, I just didn't have papa to cook for, so I didn't cook at all. I didn't know I was hungry 'til now."

"There isn't any cornbread left, but you can carve off some of that buffalo meat and sit by the fire with us an' talk."

Minerva sliced some meat into a tin plate, then joined us by the fire. She had only begun to eat when Billy slipped into the firelight looking for all the world like a warrior, save he wore no warpaint.

Minerva froze. If I've ever seen terror in someone's eyes, it was in her eyes as she stared at Billy. Having lived among white people for so long Billy knew that Minerva was thinking he was a savage. He wasn't a'goin' to disappoint her.

Billy glanced at Mama and poured out a rapid sentence in Shoshone. We didn't know what Billy said, but we had to live with him, so we played along. Billy repeated his request in sign language and broken English.

"Trade!" he said.

"You want to trade?" Mama questioned.

"Yes. Trade!"

"What do you want?"

"Squaw," he said.

"Squaws are terribly expensive," Mama said. "Would you consider trading for something else?"

"Me want 'em squaw! Want young squaw with good teeth for softening buckskin."

A mischievous streak I hadn't seen before got the best of Mama and she started to dicker.

"The little one isn't for trade, 'cause she's not mine. You'll have to settle for the grown girl," Mama said, indicating me.

"Mother!" I protested. "How could you!" It was difficult to keep a straight face.

Billy grunted and looked me over from head to toe. It made me nervous.

"One horse," he said at last.

"One horse isn't nearly enough," Mama said in mock surprise. "She's worth at least ten horses."

"No squaw worth ten horses!"

"This one is worth ten horses," Mama protested, "though there are times when I'd give her away."

"Mother!" I said, stamping my foot. "Please! "

Minerva's eyes were big and round and full of horror. Billy feigned anger and reached for an arrow. "Five horses!" he said. "No more. She's missed too many meals."

"I'm as healthy as any other squaw you'd ever find!" I yelled, feigning anger.

"You don't want Mae for a squaw, Billy," Hector spoke from under the wagon. Minerva jumped, not knowing Hector existed. "She'd make you wash your ears before meals. It's better you keep the five horses."

"Can't buy her anyway, White Eyes," Billy admitted.

"Why not?" I broke in.

"Don't have five horses."

"Wh . . . what's going on?" Minerva timidly asked.

"Mama just about sold me to Billy," I said. "But my little brother had to spoil it."

"You mean he's a tame Indian?" Minerva asked.

"I wouldn't call him *tame*," I said. "But he's handy to have around. With him, life isn't dull."

Minerva looked bewildered.

"Billy," I said, "I'd like you to meet Minerva Tally. Minerva, this is Billy Harold."

"It's a pleasure to meet you, ma'am," Billy said as he bowed. Minerva didn't know what to think.

"I'm Julienne Brisk," Mama said. "This is Mae Brisk, and the lad under the wagon is Hector Brisk. Now that you have been properly introduced, why don't you finish your supper?"

We were two teenage girls thrown together by circumstances, Minerva and I. Though we didn't always see eye-to-eye, we enjoyed each other's company.

Minerva had a heavy wagon, pulled by two span of big, fine-looking Missouri mules. Dirty blue with orange wheels, the ten-year-old wagon was well preserved. Though not as large as a Conestoga, when new it could have been considered a luxury prairie schooner.

The wagon canvas was new, or had been when their journey started. Unless I missed my guess, there was a spare bolt of canvas tucked away somewhere in her wagon. Outfitted with all the tools of a competent prospector, there was a place for everything, and everything was in it's place. Minerva's father had known what he was doing.

As far as I knew, Minerva didn't ask permission to travel with us. She just harnessed up and fell in beside us when we pulled out the next morning. She was young but this was a land for growing up fast and she didn't look like a helpless little girl atop her wagon seat, workin' those big mules.

"There's dust ahead," Billy noted one morning. "Whoever they are, they're traveling west a few miles ahead of us."

"You mean we're catching up with a wagon train?" Minerva questioned. "Unless they've been camped, my wagon train should be nearly a week in front of us."

"Come nightfall I'll ride up and see who they are," Billy said. "Til then we best keep our own dust down."

Minerva looked at him, shocked. More 'n likely it'd never occurred to her that there was danger from anyone 'cept Indians. From then on we drove slower, keeping our wheels on the grass, raising as little dust as possible.

When the dust ahead of us disappeared, I thought I saw a worried look on Billy's face. If Billy was worried, it must be serious. I fetched my revolver, strapping the holster under my dress, and Mama checked the load in Papa's shotgun. Minerva looked bewildered but checked her own weapon too.

A rattlesnake startled Minerva's mules and one of them started bucking in it's harness. When one mule starts bucking in the harness the whole team gets panicky, so Minerva had her hands full.

Billy nudged his Appaloosa to the mule's side to assist in soothing the animal. Even with his help it took five, maybe six minutes to calm down the team. Dust billowed up obscuring everyone's vision.

With all the dust and excitement we didn't see the men approach, but suddenly there they were—seven of 'em . . . ugly and unwashed and holding guns. Recognizing two of the men as the horse thieves, Mama defiantly met the gaze of the leader.

Harry nudged his horse forward. "You're the widow woman from the prairie," he accused, spitting the words as if they were something ugly. "You spread stories 'bout Mel and me in Steady."

"No I didn't, but I wish I had! You're no-account horse thieves!" Mama declared.

"Could be," Harry replied, easy-like. "But your stories got Tex and Smith lynched."

"They weren't lynched, they were legally hanged! They deserved it, too!"

"Could be," Harry grunted in a mild voice. "But what you're about to get, you deserve, too."

"You surely do!" Mel added.

"My friend and I thought highly of Tex and Smith." Harry spoke like a judge giving verdict. "We just can't let their hanging go unrevenged."

One man flipped Billy's Smith and Wesson from his holster. We were in trouble, big trouble.

A horse stomped, and the men grinned. Oh, they were enjoying themselves, they surely were. I looked to Billy's face and saw nothing, nothing at all. I didn't believe even Billy could get us out of this one.

Suddenly the outlaws grew tense, turning their heads in the breeze as if trying to hear something.

No one spoke. A horse blew. Billy's mare pranced nervously, yet a-purpose, I suspect, as it was unlike her.

Then I heard it too—a chant, low and ominous. The chanting grew louder and the eyes of the seven flashed, nervously. Suddenly I realized that in the midst of her nervous prance, Billy's mare had backed out from between the two riders that flanked her.

A quick move from Billy, and his Arkansas toothpick flashed across the tight circle to bury itself in the chest of the malcontent directly opposite. At almost that same instant Papa's double barreled shotgun seemed to materialize into Mama's hand, and bellowed. I never saw her reach for it.

A horse screamed and a Shoshone war cry filled the morning air, delivering terror and making hair stand on end. Several horses were bucking, having been burned by a stray buckshot. Minerva's mules, skittish from the snake, were again bucking in their traces, but Minerva was taking care of them.

The suddenness and ferocity of Billy's attack frightened me. It was a side of him I didn't know existed.

I slid my hand into the rip in my skirt for my own weapon. As I fetched it I was vaguely aware that Billy was off his mare, kneeling on one knee, repeatedly fitting arrows to his bowstring, an' letting 'em fly.

One of the men had circled around behind Billy and was drawing a bead with his pistol.

"Billy!" I yelled. Closing my eyes I fired my pistol in the general direction of the desperado. When I opened my eyes the man's horse had fallen and he was jumping onto another horse that was running by.

Three men wheeled their mounts and raked their spurs brutally across the animals' flanks. Like a shot, the animals jumped to, taking the riders to the safety of the prairie. Three other mounts followed with empty saddles.

Snatching a pistol from a downed man . . . his own pistol, Billy leaped into his mare's saddle and gave chase.

Suddenly all was still, save the drumming of hooves in the background. A horse blew and dust settled. Billy was gone and on the ground were four bodies. One had Billy's knife in his heart and two had been killed with arrows. The fourth man had been cut down by Mama's shotgun. Have you ever seen what a shotgun blast can do to a man, when taken at five yards in the chest? It had near cut 'im in two. Minerva looked upon the man's remains and sickened. Moments later she was off in the sagebrush, vomiting.

"What happened?" Mama asked.

"It was a chant," I said. "A Shoshone chant came in the wind."

"What are you talking about, Mae?"

"Didn't you hear it?" I asked.

"I saw the men actin' almighty strange, but I didn't hear nothing."

"I didn't hear nothin' either," said Hector. "I wish I had!"

Since it seemed nobody else heard it, I decided not to press the issue.

The sound of hooves in the distance drew our attention. It was Billy, driving three horses with empty saddles toward us. They were the horses of three of the dead men.

Billy rode to the wagon, drew rein, and dismounted. Examining each body, he grunted.

"Mel and Harry are not among the dead," he said. "We still have them to contend with." He looked over at the dead horse. "I didn't have nothing against the horse," he said.

I looked down a little bit ashamed.

"Mae," he said. I looked up and saw him smiling. "I owe you one."

If anything I owed him fifty, but he spoke so sincerely. With the excitement and the killing, I was surprised when I finally noticed my cheeks were wet. Mama squeezed me and said, "There's no shame in crying over a scene like this.

We dug graves on the rise near the river and buried the dead. The graves were not deep, but adequate. Though Billy pitched in and helped with the graves, I noticed he didn't seem to have his heart in it. He probably would have been for chucking the bodies in a shallow draw away from the trail and caving dirt in atop them. But I guess he'd learned to give us womenfolk our way in some things.

Hard and long I looked at Billy. What manner of man was he? Remembering the chant, I wondered what sort of relationship he had with his dead father. He had said something about a spirit world where the dead go, but I didn't understand. The idea of a spirit world seemed strange, yet comforting. If'n there really was a spirit world, that's where my Pa would be.

• Chapter Twelve •

Mae

Papa would have been proud of the way we stood up to the malevolent element. It always puzzled me how he, usually a peaceful man, hated to miss a good scrap. It goes to show that you never really understand another person, even when you live all your life with him.

As we drove west life seemed good. At last we were on the Oregon trail; the hardest part of our journey was behind us. Yep, Oregon or bust!

We were just a-moseying along at the oxen's rate, when we saw a prairie fire to the southwest darkening the sun with it's smoke. Maybe it was an accident . . . I don't know. Maybe it was set a-purpose by Harry, Mel, or their third partner. Billy thought it was set on purpose. *Our* purpose was to get out of harm's way.

A prairie fire can travel as fast as the wind blows or at least as fast as the wind can tumble a dry weed. No more than half a mile to our right was the Platte River. But a half mile can be a long ways with a prairie fire nipping at your heels. Then, too, this time o' year the Platte wasn't much more than a stream—not a formidable barrier for a prairie fire.

No one gave the order. We just turned as one and raced to the river. Ten or fifteen minutes is all we could hope for, and that's not much time. No trees lined the banks at this part of the river. The prairie terminated in a sheer two foot drop to the water's surface. It was high enough to break a wagon wheel.

While the rest of us looked for a spot to ease the wagons into the water, Billy tested the depth of the river and found it as deep as his stirrups. We finally caved in the bank using mining tools from Minerva's wagon and made a crude ramp.

To our disappointment, even in the deepest part of the river, the water was barely deep enough to wet the bottoms of the wagon boxes. We drove to the far side of the river and started throwing buckets of water on the canvas.

Our oiled canvas tended to shed water rather than get wet through-and-through. The oiled canvas made our plight all the more dangerous; oiled canvas burns like tinder. Minerva's canvas had been rubbed with animal fat and bees wax, which makes it burn equally well as oiled canvas.

Billy tied a buckskin shirt over his Appaloosa's eyes. The rest of us took cue from him and tied something, anything we could find, over the eyes of all the animals. Then Minerva started spreading wet blankets over her mules. Smart girl, I thought. We did the same with our animals. Then we hobbled the animals as they stood in the water. But no matter how much you prepare, you can never be fully prepared for a prairie fire.

With a roar the fire came. It came very fast and was almighty hot. We just huddled in the safety of the water.

You would not have expected the Platte River to turn a prairie fire, but it did. Rather than jumping the river, the fire veered to the east, slowly losing it's momentum.

"Guess the river stopped the fire," Minerva commented when it was safe to look around.

"A river this narrow won't stop a fire that large," Billy grunted.

"But it did!" she objected. "You saw it!"

"I saw it all right, but more 'n likely it was stopped by the God of the Mormons."

"What do you mean?" Minerva asked.

"There's a Mormon company not many miles to the north. That company would have been wiped out had the fire continued.

"I haven't seen any Mormons," Mama said.

"I've been seeing dust for days," answered Billy.

Minerva shuttered. "I don't trust Mormons."

"Why not?" Billy asked.

"Heard too many bad stories of 'em."

"Have you ever met one?"

"No," she admitted.

"Regardless of the stories you've heard," Billy said, "It would be safer to be with them than out here where Mel or Harry can burn us out."

"Well . . . I . . . I still don't like it."

"Course, maybe the Mormons won't have *you*, Minerva," Billy stated, face stoic. I suspected he was teasing Minerva.

"Why not?"

"Could be they might not trust you. You're from Missouri, right?"

"Right."

"Your Missouri militia, under Governor Boggs, tried to exterminate the Mormons. Seems the Mormons didn't take too kindly to extermination."

"That's not the way I heard it back in Missouri," Minerva defended herself. "I heard the Mormons were abolitionists and traitors."

"Nevertheless, Minerva, they might not take kindly to you."

"Look here, Billy, are you a Mormon lover?"

"Minerva," I spoke up firmly, unable to hide my amusement. "Billy *is* a Mormon."

Yes siree, you could o' knocked Minerva over with a feather. Her mouth gaped open, then she turned to Billy and stammered, "But you're an Indian."

"So you noticed," Billy replied in amusement.

"I . . . I mean, I didn't know Indians could be Mormons."

"Ever heard of the Book of Mormon?"

"You mean the Mormon's gold Bible?"

"Yes."

"I've heard of it."

"It features my Indian ancestors."

Minerva was dumbfounded. She realized she wasn't making a positive impression with the young Shoshone who seemingly held her destiny in his hands.

"We'll drive to the Mormon wagon company and spend the night with 'em," Billy announced. "From there you can decide if you want to travel with them, if'n they'll have you."

We didn't have much of a choice, 'cause the Mormon's would have to be mighty bad company to be worse than the horse thieves. So we agreed. Still, it was a scary thought, 'cause *we* surely weren't Mormons either.

Losing no time, we whipped up our teams and turned their heads north. In an hour we reached the Mormon Trail, and followed it west. Dust from the recent wagon train hung heavy in the air, so we knew we were not far behind.

Several hours passed. We knew we were gaining, as the smell of dust was stronger. "They aren't traveling very fast," Minerva commented.

"Mormon wagon companies have to travel slow, 'cause most everyone walks," Billy explained.

"Even the children?" I put in.

"All 'cept babies," Billy confirmed. "There isn't much riding space, as their wagons are always loaded full of furniture and the like."

The Mormon encampment was in sight, and we were all a little concerned . . . all but Billy. We were not part of them; we were "gentiles" from what Billy said, and didn't belong.

A party of four mounted men separated themselves from the encampment and rode toward us. I didn't like it, but it was only common sense for them to find out who we were and what we wanted.

We stopped our wagons and waited for them to reach us. I busied myself adjusting my hair and Mama brushed her dress. But Minerva did nothing, she just sat atop her wagon seat and gawked.

The four riders bucked their mounts to a stop. Dust billowed into the air, as we were on the powder dry trail.

"Sorry ma'am," the leader spoke in a Southern accent. "We raised a mite more dust than we intended."

"It's okay," Mama said graciously. "When you drive over heavily traveled wagon trails, you have to accept dust."

The leader looked at Billy, and there was recognition in his eyes. "Well, Billy," he said, "ya'll going to introduce us to the ladies?" We all looked at Billy, as we hadn't considered that he might know the wagon master.

"Brother Flake, may I introduce Julienne Brisk, her lovely daughter Mae, and Mae's brother, Hector. On the wagon seat is Minerva Tally." Then turning to us he continued, "This is Bill Flake from Parowan, Utah. He'll have to introduce the other gentlemen 'cause I don't know them."

"Samuel Hyde, Cain Pratt, and Ezra Campbell," Flake offered. We exchanged polite greetings.

"Minerva and her papa were on their way to the gold fields but were set by the side of the trail by a wagon master who figured Mr. Tally, who had infection in his leg, should die in peace, bless his soul."

"Sorry for your misfortune, Miss Tally," Flake offered.

"Ain't no call to be sorry, Mr. Flake. Papa and I are from Missouri, and his death is my misfortune, not yours."

I was embarrassed at her brass. Flake looked into her eyes trying to figure her. Minerva lowered her gaze to her mules.

"I found the Brisk family stranded out on the prairie," Billy said, breaking the tension. "They had been stranded by a group of self-styled badmen."

Flake lifted his eyebrows curiously.

"They were horse thieves who swiped the Brisk's mules while the Brisks were traveling alone on the Texas panhandle. The thieves said the mules were the only thing of value the Brisks had.

"But it seems," Billy continued, "the horse thieves came by misfortune themselves. Two of them got themselves invited to a neck-tie party staged by the town fathers at Steady, Colorado. Another thief lost his hair in an Indian raid out on the prairie."

"Noticed you have some horses with empty saddles."

"Well, Brother Flake . . . seems the two remaining horse thieves found new friends and set them upon us. But they learned that in battle it doesn't pay to underestimate your opponent."

"The horses, I suppose, belong to the horse thieves' friends?"

"Oh, no sir! The horses *used* to belong to the horse thieves' friends. Now that Julienne and I have counted coup over our enemies, the horses belong to us . . . or rather to me. It's an Indian tradition, you know."

"I know," Flake grinned. "I also know you'll do justice to the story, and I can hardly wait to hear it." The three men chuckled, and the sound made me feel good.

"Brother Campbell will show you to your camping spot," Flake added, almost as an afterthought. "Let's get back before we miss supper." He wheeled his mount, and set a course to the Mormon encampment.

• CHAPTER THIRTEEN •

Mae

Mama and I watched and listened, trying to learn all we could about the Mormon wagon train. We learned that Mormon wagon companies are different from other wagon trains we'd seen. They have a company captain or wagon master and a captain over every ten wagons. They were well ordered villages on wheels. You either function as part of the rolling village or you don't travel with the Mormons; they tolerate no loners.

As Billy said, Mormon wagons are filled so full with everything imaginable that, except for the old, lame, and babies, everyone walks. One young couple pulled a handcart. A middle aged man walked on a wooden leg. There was room for him to ride, but he said it was a joy to be independent.

"You have been assigned to my section," Ezra Campbell informed us after the evening meal. "That is," he hedged, "if you choose to travel with us."

"What will be expected of us?" Mama asked. It was something we all wanted to know, especially Minerva.

"Hector will be assigned to the fire and water detail with the other boys his age. Mae will milk one of your cows—"

"What about the other cow?" asked Mama, somewhat suspicious.

"I was a comin' to that. The Alborne family's cow dried up, and we would like to talk you into loaning your second cow to the Albornes in exchange for flour. Billy said you don't have any wheat flour." Hector grinned. It'd been a month of Sundays since we'd had wheat flour.

"You, Mrs. Brisk, would be responsible for your family's cooking and laundry, but you would share a fire with four other families." Mama raised her eyebrows.

"We don't want to burn up all the buffalo chips," Campbell explained. "There isn't much to burn out here on the prairie, as you know, and there are wagon companies traveling behind us. So we use group fires and only burn what we need, leaving fuel for others."

"Makes sense," Mama said, "though I hadn't thought of it that way." She was impressed. So was I.

"Minerva," Campbell said, turning her way. "If you choose to travel with us, we'd like you to help the Martin family when you're not busy with your own team and wagon. Sister Martin has been ill, and Brother Martin is captain of the guards, which gives him the duty of protecting us all. They have five young'uns, and could use your help with the cooking while she gets on her feet again. Fact is, your help will be Godsend to them."

Minerva nodded, not fully convinced she wanted to do this, but willing to try. What else could she do?

"Are the arrangements satisfactory with all of you?" he asked, finalizing the conversation. He looked to each of us, even Hector, and we all nodded our consent.

"It's time to get ready for the evening program," he announced, as he was taking his leave. "Tonight will be dancing. It starts in fifteen minutes."

"I didn't know Mormons danced." I commented to Mama when Campbell was out of hearing range.

"Neither did I," she replied.

As I returned to my task of putting the supper dishes away, my eyes met the eyes of a boy several wagons away. Blushing I quickly returned to my work. A strange thrill gripped me.

As I was completing my tasks, I sensed someone standing near me. It was Billy. "Ready for the dance?" he asked.

"Do we have to change into Sunday-go-to-meeting clothes?" I inquired.

"No, come as you are." He offered me his arm, as a Southern gentleman might. I took it, and he escorted me to the dance circle.

The whole camp was there, 'cept those on guard duty. My eye caught the eye of the boy I'd seen earlier. He was watching me. He was standing with a girl that looked much like him, maybe a sister. Never in my whole life had I been around so many people my age. All these people in one place was scary, but I decided I could learn to like traveling with the Mormons. A feeling of excitement gripped me.

Old and young, everyone danced. A dance caller called and a fiddler fiddled. It was square dancing, save a few dances that they called "minuets," something I'd never heard of before."

The boy who had caught my eye earlier slid to my side. I was very conscious of his presence.

"I'm Edward," he offered. He was very handsome.

"I'm Mae," I replied. We danced. He didn't exactly ask me to dance, but in square dancing you naturally find yourself dancing with every man in your square, even if it's just for a brief swing.

"I'm Ellen, Edward's twin sister," a girl introduced herself between dances. "The others in the square are Rolando, Rufus, Clarica, Angus, Josephine, and of course you know Billy." We said our how-dee-doos, and suddenly I had friends . . . friends my age. They may have been Mormons, but at least they were friends. I guess the need for friendship and acceptance knows no religion.

The world was beautiful.

Every night there was an activity and I had great fun with my new friends. Yet I yearned for Billy Harold. To my concern, he hadn't become part of the wagon company but roamed on his spotted Appaloosa thither and yon. Now and again he came in for a meal but didn't stay long. It was said he was serving Captain Flake as a scout.

"You love him, don't you?" Mama said one afternoon as we walked along. I guess I had been lost in thought.

"Love who?" I pretended I didn't know.

"Billy, of course. Every time an Appaloosa gets close you strain to see if Billy is in the saddle."

Suddenly my eyes were hot and tears close to the surface. "Mama, I'm sorry. I know I wasn't suppose to fall in love with him—with an Indian. What'll I do?"

Mama put her arm around me and drew me to her as we walked. "Sometimes only time can heal an aching heart," she said, and there was a catch in her voice. "I . . . I thought I couldn't go on without Jedediah . . . but . . . I had to."

It seemed clear that there was no thought in her mind but that Billy and I would part company. It didn't hardly seem fair, but what other alternative was there?

One day we came under attack by buffalo. Billy had ridden in hell-bent-for-leather and had a hasty conference with Flake.

"Corral!" Captain Flake yelled, and his orders were echoed by the captains of ten. We were told it had something to do with the buffalo. We'd seen buffalos about and were delighted because of the prospects of meat. The beasts had nearly disappeared from the Oregon Trail, which was just across the river.

We circled our wagons, then Flake gave orders to slap ropes, chains, hobbles, or whatever we had, on all the animals. I surely didn't know what was going on, neither did most of the Mormons. But we did as we were told.

"If the buffaloes get among our cattle," Ezra Campbell explained to his group of ten wagons, "when they leave, the domestic cattle will go with 'em. Horses will sometimes go with 'em too. It's the call of the herd.

"The domestic animals won't stay with the herd very long, only for a few days," he continued. "But by then they may be a hundred miles away. Chances are, once cattle get in a buffalo herd the owners will never find 'em again."

The herd came by, and we stood by our animals. The

buffaloes tried to get among the wagons, but there were no
holes.

As the herd thinned, the hunters went out, trying for
blunt horns but willing to harvest anything less than full
grown. They shot meat for the whole camp and all shared.
The buffalo robes went to whoever wanted to tan them, but
none were wasted. "Three hundred miles back, we couldn't
have harvested this much buffalo meat," Campbell said.

"Why not?" Minerva asked.

"There wasn't enough room to carry the cured meat or
the weight and bulk of the robes. But since then, hundreds
of pounds of grain have been consumed from each wagon.
So now the Lord has blessed us with more food."

To the Mormons, the meat represented a feast now and
cured meat for weeks to come. But to us Brisks who had
eaten much meat, thanks to Billy's marksmanship, just
being with the Mormons and eating breadstuff was treat
enough. But we did enjoy the fresh meat, as what we
brought with us was smoked or dried.

With the buffalo also came our first real contribution to
the wagon company, as our wagon was temporally loaded
heavy with freight displaced from wagons that needed room
for meat. For a few days there was no question of Mama
walking, though she usually walked anyway, 'cause all the
Mormon women were walking, 'cept on down-hill stretches.
Most wagon's brakes were on the right, so you walked on
the right of the team, often with a rope in your hand that
was tied to the tip of the brake pole.

We'd been with the Mormons for weeks, and I have to
say this for 'em: They sure know how to put a wagon train
together and make traveling pleasant, or as pleasant as
possible. Fact is, I was dreading the day we would part.

Whenever I thought of parting with my Mormon friends
in the wagon company, I thought of parting with Billy, and
a gloom overtook me. I was in love with him and knew it. I
had to find a way to fall out of love with him, as there
seemed no chance of marrying him.

Our section was third in traveling order, and we were the fourth wagon in our section of ten wagons, making us the twenty-fourth wagon in the train of more than a hundred wagons. With this much dust near the front of the column, I wondered what it was like near the rear? We were coming into August and a good rain was sorely needed to help settle the dust.

Edward fell in step beside me. His ruggedly handsome face and easy manners took the edge off my heartaches for Billy.

"We haven't seen much but sand and wild sagebrush for three hundred miles," he commented, making easy conversation. "Brother Flake said the scenery will soon change."

"I surely hope so," I replied.

"In a way, the scenery has already changed," he went on. "It changed the day you arrived."

I blushed, liking his words but trying not to let it show. It was fun being with a young man my age.

"Where is your family from, Edward?" I asked, making conversation myself.

"Liverpool. That's in England."

"You mean you came all the way from England just to walk across these prairies?"

"We came from England to gather with the Saints in Utah," he corrected me.

"Why is that so important?"

"Because we're different. Everybody that serves the Lord is different. The Pilgrims were different, the Methodists were different, and the followers of Martin Luther were different. It's different to put your heart and soul into any religion."

"I see."

"Course," he hedged, "the good Lord made everyone different in one way or another."

"Yes," I replied, thinking of Billy.

When we reached Laramie I thought Minerva might choose to leave the Mormon company in favor of a gentile wagon train, but she didn't. Laramie was a wide open town where everything was too expensive. It wasn't much of a place to look at either. This is where we would have met up with the Oregon Trail had we still been with Jackman, though we would have been coming from the south, through Cherry Creek.

I looked for Billy, but he was not around, and it briefly angered me. But it was just as well Billy wasn't around 'cause my hankering for him needed to cool down.

From Laramie we started a three hundred mile climb to South Pass. The Rocky Mountains, rugged and high elsewhere, gave way along this section of the trail to the swell of the Great Plains. The trail was powder dry. When it was windy the dust blew in rolling clouds. When there was no breeze at all, the dust floated in the air much like fog.

In the stillness of a hot afternoon I shuffled along the trail kicking up dust with every step. With my bonnet pulled low over my eyes and a scarf around my mouth to breathe through, I must have looked a sight. A glance at Hector and I laughed in spite of myself. His bandanna covered his whole face and he looked like a walking dust ball.

"What's ya laughing at, Mae?"

"*You* . . . covered head to toe with dust . . . an' no face," I chuckled.

"I got a face," he said, lifting his bandanna, "but I'm sure glad the oxen are watching the trail." Then changing the subject he pointed to the low, rolling hills. "Look! There's Billy!"

I almost looked, trapped by his playful teasing. "Is he a dust ball or a cloud?" I teased back.

"Serious, Mae," he insisted. "There's Billy, leading his mare."

I looked. Sure enough, there *was* Billy, leading the Appaloosa by a halter rope. The horse was being used as a pack animal, piled high with what appeared to be parts of furniture. I quickly straightened my dress, brushing the dust from me as best I could.

"Looks like you're walking drag today," Billy observed, to no one in particular.

"At least there is a river close at hand so we can wash up at the end of the day. Tomorrow we will rotate to the head of the column," I replied.

"What's your horse a-packin'?" Hector asked.

"Parts of furniture . . . a rocking chair and chest of drawers, for Brother Flake," he grinned.

"I don't get it." I said.

"Well," Billy began, "when immigrants to Oregon leave the Missouri River, they don't realize how far 2,000 miles is. As they get into this climb to South Pass with its thinning air, they realize they have to do something or their team will give out 'cause they're loaded too heavily for mountain travel."

"I can see that," I put in.

"So, they start looking for things to cast off," Billy continued. "Course the first things to go are the empty food barrels. The next thing is the furniture that is falling apart."

"Falling apart?" I questioned.

"Immigrants are often coming from a wet climate. Much of the furniture dries up and the joints become loose, and it starts to squeak as it bounces along in the wagon bed. So when they have to lighten their load, they choose the dried-up squeaky furniture to cast off.

"In Utah, the Mormon's have lots of craftsman but little hardwood. So if there is room in the wagons, the Mormon companies have taken to sending out scouts to spot and pick up the cast off hardwood furniture. Then it's remade. It's common to find a few pieces of elegant, hardwood furniture in the most humble Mormon homes."

He tied the halter rope to the rear of the wagon, and Billy walked along beside me. In the dust our fingers touched. There was just a moment's hesitation, then he took my hand in his. We didn't say a word. There wasn't anything to say. We just walked through the clouds of dust, making our way with squinted eyes. I felt warm inside like I've never felt before. It wasn't an Indian I was a-holdin' hands with, or even a Mormon. It was Billy, the man I loved.

That evening Billy took supper with us. But the next

morning I looked out from my under-the-wagon bed to see
Billy pulling out. He was trailing one of the horse thieves'
horses. He cast a glance at our wagon, I'll have to give him
that, but it was no way near a proper good-bye. Then he
was gone.

• CHAPTER FOURTEEN •

Billy

Low on my Appaloosa's back, I rode like the wind. Behind me I trailed a long legged roan gelding that looked like it had speed and stamina. I brought it so I could change horses while on the move. I had a long way to go, and Brother Flake said that if I were to return to the wagon company before they reached Bridger, I'd have to move fast and hard.

At Bridger the Brisks would depart the company, and I'd never see them again. Unless . . . but I just wasn't sure.

I was heading for the Shoshone village, at least to the spot where the village had been when I was a boy. There I would attempt to commune with the Great Spirit, or God, as the Mormon in me called him. My white father, who was raised by the Pawnees, called him Ti-rá-wa.

Hourly I switched mounts, traveling at a mile-eating pace. When traveling to and from raids, back when we were a large tribe—a tribe to be reckoned with—Shoshone warriors traveled this way, sometimes both day and night. They even slept on their horses while moving, though at least one warrior had to remain awake to guide.

Once I saw an eagle hesitate in its flight, circle, then return the way it came. Quickly I took to a draw, secluded my mounts in some juniper trees, and snaked out for a look. It was a party of Utes, not whites, though it made no difference to me. I slipped around them and continued on my way.

Into the night I rode. I watched my horse's ears 'cause their hearing is better than mine. If given their choice, most Indians will stay away from night travel, but trained by my mountain man father, I have no such inhibitions. Still, man and animal need rest, so when I found a likely spot with water and good grass, I picketed my horses and curled up in a deer bed for some sleep.

It was not the travel time that caused me to hurry; it was the fasting time. White men, even Mormons, often give their prayers a lick-and-a-promise. But to us Lamanites it's serious business.

I traveled nigh onto twenty hours a day for three-and-a-half days. I knew it wouldn't take me nearly so long to return 'cause the wagon company would have had a week's travel in my general direction during my absence.

When I reached the village site, I slowed my mounts to a reverent walk. The site was overgrown, but my Shoshone parents' wickiup still stood. I'd rebuilt it most every year since Brigham adopted me, ten years ago. It was Brigham who showed me where the site was. That was the first summer after he adopted me. He had brought me here to commune with the Great Spirit.

I purified myself and put on garments made of animal skins. I gave credit to the four winds and the six directions, and gave thanks to my strength, my family, my village, my tribe, and I added a fifth . . . my Mormon religion. Maybe I'm wrong . . . I don't know . . . but I can see no conflict between my Indian and my white man's religion.

"Great Spirit," I prayed, hands outstretched to heaven. "I wish to take a woman . . . the white eyes named Mae. Her hair is the color of a buffalo robe, and her eyes are as pools of blue water. Her heart is pure, and in her hands she holds my heart."

For three days I fasted and prayed for a vision, 'cause that is the tradition. I chanted the chants taught me from my youth and prayed the prayers of my white training. After the three days, my soul was putty in the hands of the Great Spirit, and I observed the Great Silence.

I sat in front of my tiny fire meditating, my bear claw necklace in my hand.

When most Indians fast, often they smoke the medicine pipe. But I don't use tobacco, 'cause I'm a Mormon. So I stared into the smoke, 'cause that is where the visions come. But it isn't always so. When my Shoshone father, Jag-en-up, appeared to me, it was not in smoke but in the clear light of the sun as I topped the rise that overlooked the Lloyd homestead.

As I sat there, observing the Great Silence, gradually I became aware of a chant not of my own utterance. In the flickering smoke I thought I saw a Shoshone maiden, young and comely. Her clarity increased until suddenly I realized she was not a maiden, but my Shoshone mother, Saw-wich. She didn't look many summers older than me. Even in my dreams I had never imagined her so beautiful. She had high cheekbones and dark, sparkling eyes; her brown round face was set off by her long, shiny hair, neatly parted in the center and loosely braided.

Her manner of dress was the way I remembered: two slightly trimmed deer hides stitched along the sides. Her arms, which had so often held me, hung gently at her side, palms forward.

I remembered her rocking me on her lap, gently singing the songs and chanting the chants of our people until she was killed by the Utes and I was taken captive. I had longed to be in her arms once again, or to look upon her lovely countenance.

"Saw-wich," I said, calling her by name. I would have gone to her, but how do you go to a spirit, hovering in the smoke of a ceremonial fire? She smiled sweetly, then spoke.

"The white maiden is beautiful." She spoke in Shoshone; her voice was beautiful, like the song of the meadowlark.

"Yes, Mother," I said, surprised that she knew why I was there. "She is beautiful. And I love her . . . but can she share my life . . . my mission, taught me by my white father, to help our people?"

"Only the Great Spirit knows."

"The Great Spirit has not imparted his knowledge to me."

"Nor to me."

"But should I take her to my lodge?"

"You must decide for yourself," she said as she started to fade from my view. "Marriage rites do not make a marriage, my son. Two people working as one make a marriage. Man and woman are only one when they work as one."

Then she was gone. Why had she faded so fast? Why do spirits always leave so soon after delivering their message? My eyes wanted to linger to help my heart remember our short time in this world together. I wanted to hear the old songs and chants from her own lips as only she could sing them.

I stared long into the smoke after she was gone. I even reached out with my hand hoping to touch something of her, but there was nothing—only the warmth of the embers as it rose into the sky. My eyes, like the great thunder-clouds, were full of water. Inside me, though, I felt a warmth like the warmth of the embers.

"Mother," I said.

I was left alone with my thoughts . . . and the fire. But I knew of what she spoke, 'cause Brigham Young had taught back in Manti that though a couple might be sealed in the Endowment House, they had to live so their marriage might be sealed by the Holy Spirit of Promise. Only then, I presumed, could a couple's mission be one.

It was late in the day and I was weak from fasting, but I had far to travel. I helped myself to several short drinks of cold water, then reached into my bag and pulled out some buffalo jerky. I stuffed a hunk into my mouth so it would soften up as I rode along.

I rode at an easy gait, forcing myself to concentrate. When weak from fasting, just as when tired from battle, it's easy to make tiny errors in judgment that can cause you to lose your scalp.

My mind wandered in spiet of my determination. I thought of my people and how they must change. Chief Sagwitch has to change; Chief Pocatello has to change; all have to change.

It was a sad day when my people stopped listening to the wise council of Chief Washakie, my father's friend. The young men started listening to Chief Pashego, a Bannock, turning their anger to the wagon trains along the Oregon trail that cross our hunting ground. Several hundred warriors, women, and children were slaughtered at the Battle of Bear River by the Black Coats. It almost silenced the Shoshone chant forever.

When the sun went down, I slept in another deer bed. I dreamed about my people at first. Then my dreams turned to the Brisks and to Mae, and then to the white thieves who were still intent on hurting them.

• CHAPTER FIFTEEN •

Mae

I shuffled along at the oxens' gait feeling more bewildered than sore over Billy's sudden departure. I forced the corners of my mouth to curve up 'cause you can't spend your whole life pouting. Yet there was an ache in my heart that watered my eyes now and again.

We were climbing to the continental divide. It was a slow, gradual climb as the prairie literally swelled into the mountains.

The day we crossed the beautiful South Pass was a day of celebration. Though I knew nothing of their religion, I began to talk like a Mormon, joke like a Mormon, and even think like a Mormon. Calling the other company members brother so-and-so or sister so-and-so became natural to me. It had been weeks since I considered the horse thieves; they were of another world.

Brother Flake struck a southwesterly course for Fort Bridger. Purchased from Jim Bridger, the remains of the old fort was owned by the Mormons, though there were many gentile shops in the little community. Brother Campbell said one whole section was gentile.

I looked for Billy daily, but it seemed like weeks since I had seen him. Then the day before we were due to pull into Bridger, he came riding in, straight and tall in his saddle. I caught my breath, and my heart fairly jumped within my breast. That irritated me because I was angry with Billy.

Face stoic, Billy rode directly to Captain Flake and exchanged greetings. Then he drifted back to our wagon. We had another hour before we camped for the night, so I was shuffling along on the brake side of our wagon, where I belonged.

"Hello, Mae," he greeted.

Chin high, I ignored him.

"Hello, Mae," he repeated.

Still I ignored him. Swishing my skirt, I stepped out smartly, doing my duty as driver, such as it was.

"Aren't you speaking to me?" he asked.

"No!" I replied.

"Why not?" he asked.

"I'm mad at you."

"Why?"

"If'n you don't know, Billy Harold, I'm not about to tell you."

"But I *don't* know," he responded.

There was no arguin' that Billy was a clever one. He had saved our lives again and again by his savvy, but for a moment I was speechless at his ignorance.

"Do you mean to tell me that you think you can just ride off without saying a word, and not make me angry?" I snapped.

"Why, Mae," he grinned, "I think you missed me."

"You're darn right I missed you," I snapped, "and I don't like it!"

"Why?"

"Why do you ask 'why' to everything? Can't you figure anything out for yourself?"

"Apparently not."

"I don't like missing you because you're a stupid savage." Oh, it hurt me to say those words. But with tears in my eyes I continued, "A big, handsome, undependable savage!"

Ignoring my emotions he said, "You're going on to Oregon and I'm going to Manti. Figured you wouldn't want to see me around."

"Well you figured wrong!" I snapped. "Besides, maybe

I've talked Mama out of going to Oregon. Maybe we're taking the Hasting's cutoff for Utah."

"Are you?" he asked. He looked me in the face and I saw something in his eyes I had only seen a couple of times before. It made me scared and excited at the same time.

"Maybe, maybe not. I'm still trying to persuade Mama."

Billy dismounted and started walking beside me, leading his Appaloosa by the reins. His arm brushed against mine and it was all I could do not to embrace him. I wished he would take my hand.

"Mae," he said softly. "What if you couldn't persuade your mother to continue to Utah? Would you go to Utah without her?"

"Depends on if there was something for me in Utah," I answered, quietly. "As far as I know now, there's nothing."

We walked on listening to the rattle of the wagon and the wind as it sighed out of the north. Our hands were so close, his knuckles brushed mine.

"Would you consider *me* 'something?'" he asked.

"What?"

"I was wondering if I could be that 'something' to you," he said, a little more boldly.

"Billy, whatever could you mean?" I asked. Billy seemed to be driving at something—something I was too afraid to guess at—and I wanted him to make himself clear.

"Dawgonit, Mae! You're not one to cut a man a little slack now, are you?"

"Perhaps if you'd just say what you mean, I might." I answered. This was the first time I'd seen Billy off balance and I was enjoying it.

"Do you mean it, about cutting me some slack?"

"Sure. If'n, that is, you say the right things," I answered.

"Well then, I was wondering . . ." he took a deep breath, ". . . if you might consider going to Manti and becoming Mrs. Billy Harold?"

Them were the right things. I couldn't walk. I couldn't walk because I couldn't see. I couldn't see because my eyes were full of tears.

"Is that a proposal, Billy?"

"It is."

I threw my arms around his neck. "I accept," I said. For a few minutes we hugged, and the wagon train continued. No doubt each family that passed, grinned . . . I don't know . . . I wasn't watching them.

"I'm glad you appreciate Billy's company," Brother Campbell said, his voice gentle, but amused. "But your wagon is traveling driverless, unless your mother or Hector has taken command. Folks prefer that teams have a driver."

"Oh," I squealed, and ran to catch up with the team that I was supposed to be driving.

Mama gave me her blessings to marry Billy. So did Hector. "Maybe Billy will teach me how to be an Indian now that he's becoming my brother," he said excitedly. Maybe he would have if'n he had time, but Mama wouldn't change her mind about going to Oregon. A strong willed person, she had dreams of her own . . . dreams that included Oregon gold.

She'd made some mighty fine friends among the Mormons of Captain Flake's wagon company, but Mama was still leery of the Mormons and the "gathering."

"It seems as though we have a problem with the weddin'," Mama said one morning, after an hour of deep thought. My heart sank 'cause I thought she was changing her mind. "Wouldn't be fit for you to travel to Utah unwed," she told me. "Yet, there's nobody here to marry you."

"There's Captain Flake. He's an elder."

"I was meaning a real preacher, like back home," Mama replied.

"Mama!" I stiffened. "We have heard Brother Flake preach, and he surely preaches like a man of God. You said so yourself!"

"So I did."

"'Sides, he's been ordained sure as the next preacher."

Mama grinned. "There's just no getting around this wedding is there, Mae?"

"But Mama, I thought you *liked* Billy," I said.

"Oh Billy's a fine man. But maybe you haven't considered how much a mother is going to miss her daughter."

But I *had* considered how much I was going to miss my mother.

The early August sun was high and hot in the sky as I thoughtfully shuffled my way to the Mormon wagons. They bustled with activity as they prepared for the final leg of their journey across the mountains to the Salt Lake Valley.

"Are you coming on to Salt Lake with us, Mae?" Ellen inquired. She always seemed to be genuinely interested in all I did. In the weeks I'd been with the company, I'd learned to love her.

"I . . . can you keep a secret?"

"I'll try."

"You don't have to keep the secret forever, just 'til we're ready to announce it publicly."

"Are you going to tell me that you and Billy are getting married?"

"How did you know?"

"Shucks, Mae, I've guessed it for weeks. Mama said she never saw a couple more in love." I blushed and Ellen laughed.

Billy stepped up beside me, though I don't know where he came from.

"Billy," I scolded. "Did anyone ever tell you that you walk as quietly as an Indian?"

"It's been mentioned."

"But I'm glad you're here. We need to talk."

"Okay. Follow me." We walked to the rotunda of horses and mules fenced in a crude corral, partly made from rope. Billy's Appaloosa and the three horses that had belonged to our attackers back on the Platte were among the animals. I thought they were the finest looking animals there.

"Mama wants to go on to Oregon," I said.

"Does she now?"

"Yes. And she doesn't want me to travel to Utah unwed."

"Guess that's the end of it then," Billy said.

I stared into his eyes, but he didn't smile. I didn't want to cry, but my eyes just kind'a filled up on their own. I turned to walk away, but before I took one step Billy grabbed my arm, spun me around, and said, "Unless, of course, we get married right here." He grinned broadly. I almost leaped into his arms. But then it occurred to me that he had just played a nasty trick on me. I pulled my arm from his grip and stomped away.

"Maybe I don't want to be married here," I said.

"What do you mean?" he called.

"Maybe I want a big church weddin' with lots of flowers and a white dress and bells and everything else that goes into a proper wedding for a white girl." I had turned to face him and had my hands on my hips.

"Is that so?" he asked.

"You're darn tootin'," I answered.

"Well maybe I want my bride in the proper Indian fashion," Billy yelled.

"And what, may I ask, is that?" I shouldn't have asked 'cause the next thing I heard was one of those terrible Shoshone war cries and Billy was a-runnin' right at me. I didn't have the presence of mind to take one step before he picked me up and slung me over his shoulder and twirled me around.

"They just capture them," he said. After a few more rounds he put down on my feet and I leaned dizzily against him.

"I'll marry you anywhere," I said, and he squeezed me tight.

"Can we get Brother Flake to perform the ceremony?" I asked, finally breaking the silence.

"Let's go ask him together. He's over at Widow Jones' wagon repairing her double tree."

Arm in arm we walked to widow Jones's wagon. Brother Flake saw us coming and started humming, "'Here Comes the Bride.'"

"Does everyone know?" I demanded.

"Let's see," he replied, and started counting on his fingers. "You know, and Billy knows. I guess that about wraps it up. You two were the last of my company to find out."

"Mama and Hector are going on to Oregon, Brother Flake."

"I'll have to speak with her about that," he said. "It's late in the season, and she ought to be thinking of wintering someplace. It's hard enough to get over those mountains into Oregon with menfolks. A lone women and a boy ought not try it this time of year."

"She won't listen."

"She's a strong willed woman."

"She doesn't want me to go to Utah with Billy, unwed."

"Sounds reasonable."

"She has agreed to have you perform our wedding before she leaves. That is, if you are willing."

"I'm willing," he replied, with a grin.

Bridger was two communities in one, a quiet Mormon settlement and a wide open Oregon Trail town. The Mormons, who owned it, burned it to keep it out of the hands of Johnston's Army ten years ago. It had been rebuilt.

The trading post in the Mormon section of town didn't have what we wanted, so Billy and I strolled to the other section. The sounds of a tin-panny piano were coming from a hastily built combination saloon and trading post, across the street. In the shade of a tree, men had gathered to chew over the day's gossip.

There, as big as life leaning against a porch post, was Harry the horse thief. He had been rolling a cigarette, but had paused, mouth open, gawking at us. His evil eyes were dark with contempt.

"How's the horse stealing business, Harry?" Billy calmly greeted.

Harry dropped the cigarette. His eyes flit left, then right, as if wanting to see if anyone was listening. A dozen people were listening and paused to consider Billy's greeting.

I knew what Harry was thinking: Something had to be done to shut Billy's mouth. Besides, Harry's honor had been challenged. In the West where deals are consummated with the shake of a hand, a man's word of honor is worth everything.

"You lying Injun!" Harry snapped as he went for his gun.

I had no idea Billy was so fast. No siree. Just a blur of his hand and he was holding his Smith and Wesson .44. Harry's gun hadn't even cleared leather. Harry froze.

The sounds of the piano stopped. Traffic came to a halt. A fly buzzed.

"You best go back to horse stealing," Billy drawled. "You're not nearly fast enough to be a gun slinger."

Everyone on the street heard. Beads of sweat rose on Harry's forehead. He touched his tongue to his dry lips.

"Where's Mel and your other horse thieving buddy?" Billy inquired, loud enough for all to hear.

"Th . . . They're not here," Harry stammered.

"If'n I were you, I'd climb into my saddle and join them, wherever they are. Unless," Billy challenged, "you want to finish drawing."

"I . . . I'm going."

Holding his hand well free of his gun, Harry turned to a fine looking horse standing nearby. Both hands on the saddle horn, he swung into the leather. Someone chuckled, but no one spoke.

I knew why Billy had let Harry go: You just don't come into a town and shoot people, even if they deserve it. Folks, nowhere, take kindly to horse thieves, but the Texas panhandle was a whole world away. Yet Billy had gone on record as calling Harry a horse thief and from now on Harry would be a marked man.

As Harry cleared the end of the street, folks started about their own business. The tin-panny piano music could again be heard. Billy had returned his pistol to its holster. He took my arm and we started for the trading post.

Like any other trading post, the dirt floor was covered with sawdust. The north half was a saloon where a piano sat on a wooden platform. It was the tin-panny piano we'd heard earlier. The south side of the room made do for a trading post.

"That was quite a show you put on out there, Billy. Was he really a horse thief?" the proprietor asked. I have ceased to be surprised at everyone knowing Billy's name. Apparently he had been through this country often, possibly in connection with his Shoshone tribe in Idaho.

"Mr. Lott, this is Mae Brisk."

"Nice to meet ya, ma'am."

"Her mother is a widow lady who had her mules stolen by Harry and his friends out on the Texas panhandle. They took all her animals and left her and her two children to die on the prairie. Two of the thieves were hung in Colorado by the local citizenry, but Harry and a couple of partners didn't get caught."

"Hanging isn't good enough for men like that," Lott declared. "But you best watch yourself, Billy. I've known you and your papa for a good many years. Brigham sets store by you and would be hell-on-wheels if'n you should get dry-gulched."

"I'm kind of partial to this old world myself. Mae and I are going to get hitched and marriage is always better if'n you're alive to enjoy it."

Lott looked me up and down, and I could feel the color coming to my face. I wondered what he was seeing.

"You could do a lot worse, Billy," Lott declared, examination complete. "She looks like a lady who would stand beside a man."

"I'm glad you approve," I said.

Lott turned his full attention to Billy. "You didn't come to this section of town to put on a show for us. What can I do for you?"

"Do you accept Union Script?"

"Yes. We see a lot of it, being located on the Oregon Trail, as we are. Course I prefer gold. Never did understand paper money. But I've had no trouble with it. What can I get for you?"

"Here are two lists. One list is for Mae's mother, the other for us."

Lott studied the lists. "I can get you most everything listed, but it'll take a while. There must be a wagon load of supplies you're asking for. It will take me an hour to fill the order. If you come back I'll have your orders ready."

"Sounds fine, but the lists aren't everything. I want Mae to pick out some store bought clothes for herself, her mother, and her brother."

I'll give this to the Mormons, they surely know how to put on a wedding. Once we announced our wedding it became a community affair.

"Just leave it to us," Brother Flake said. "Everyone loves a wedding. It reminds all the old folks of when they were young and it fills the young'uns with expectations. It's good for the whole company."

Though the company's stay in Bridger was short, they set to work making my wedding special. A freight wagon was unloaded and the full crates used as a stage.

Out of one wagon, a piano was carried. Yes siree, a real piano. And could they ever make it talk! You never saw so much talent in all your days.

One sister fetched a lovely white wedding dress. "Wore it myself," she offered, "when I was your age."

Come time for the wedding, Billy stood on the crate stage as straight and tall as a soldier. He wore a black broadcloth suit and a white shirt with a black string tie.

Beside Billy was Mama. In the preacher's position was Brother Flake. My escort was Brother Campbell. He escorted me up the outdoor aisle to the majestic strains of "Bridal Chorus." Someone said the music was from Richard Wagner's 1848 opera *Lohengrin*, but I wouldn't know about that. I would'a marched in to "Camp Town Ladies" if that's what they played.

I took my position beside Billy, and Brother Flake stepped in front of us to begin the ceremony. The wedding ring that Billy slipped on my finger was carved from wood, but it was gold to me.

As Brother Flake pronounced us man and wife, I was vaguely aware of Mama's muffled sobs beside me. Through

Indian fights and attacks by desperados, Mama never shed
a tear. Yet at her daughter's wedding she cried like a baby.

Our wedding night was spent in a round canvas tent
which Billy purchased from the trading post. The tent was
our first home, and as far as I was concerned, no bride had
better.

In the darkness I lay in Billy's arms. My thoughts were
on Billy—on us and our future. I thought that Billy was
asleep, but then I heard, soft and low, an Indian chant. I as-
sumed it was Billy, but my ear was against his chest and he
was making no sound.

I started to open my mouth to question but Billy gently
touched my lips in a bid for silence. He pulled me closer to
him, and we listened. I didn't understand the words of the
chant, but I could tell they were joyful. They sent tingles up
my spine and filled my heart with happiness.

"Am I accepted?" I whispered.

"They are happy," Billy whispered.

"Are we going to Utah with Captain Flake's company?" I
asked Billy, come morning.

"I'm long overdue in Manti, Mae, and wagon trains
travel slowly. We don't have a wagon, so I propose we sell
the extra saddles and use the horses as pack animals."

"It sounds okay with me," I replied. "Three pack horses
should handle everything we own."

"Then it's settled," he said.

"Yes, but now that I am your wife, I have another question to ask. Where did you get the Union Script to pay for
the supplies?"

Billy grinned. "You recall the battle with the deserters at
the Cheyenne village?"

"How could I forget it? I was never so frightened in my
whole life."

"You noticed afterwards that the Cheyenne looted the
bodies of the deserters?"

I nodded, preferring not to think about it.

"Well, they didn't take the money. When they were stripping the deserters' bodies of everything of value, they discarded anything made of paper, which included paper money. There was a lot of it, many thousands of dollars worth. I gathered it up."

"Thousands of dollars? You mean we're rich?" I asked.

"Mae," Billy said gently, looking into my soul. "My Shoshone tribe needs that money more than you and I. The Oregon Trail cuts across our hunting ground, but we can't move because the rest belongs to the Paiutes, Crows, Blackfeet, or Utes. There's not enough food for my people. In the cold of winter sometimes they leave babies out at night so they'll freeze to death or be killed by wolves. That way they won't have to suffer a slow death by starvation.

"Last summer a peace treaty was signed in Bridger, which will help. But they also need help from us and that money. Weeks ago, the first day we were with the Mormon company, I packaged most of the script and entrusted it to Brother Flake to deposit in the bank in Salt Lake City. Over the years I'll draw from that account to provide food, medicine, and education for my tribe."

I was ashamed of myself . . . ashamed of my inner feelings of greed. I guess Billy sensed it 'cause he drew me to him and just held me.

"But we're not poor, Mae," he whispered. "I also have some gold. Brother Flake allowed me to tuck it into a freight wagon. He will take it on to Utah for us."

We said our good-byes and left at night. Hector hung onto me, burying his head in my hair, his body shaking with quiet sobs. He seemed strangely small and helpless. We'd been through so much together. He'd scarcely known a day without me.

Then Mama bid farewell, with tears wet and hot. Though we would write, this was possibly our last farewell on earth. She, too, seemed small and helpless and was fresh out of parental counsel.

I loved Billy, but when we rode off I thought my heart would break. I chanted my own chant to keep my courage up,

Therefore shall a woman
leave her mother and brother,
and shall cleave unto her husband,
and they shall be one flesh.

The cool of the night was in sharp contrast to the heat of
the day. I pulled my cloak around me and rode on. A lone
fox yapped in the distance and the pungent odor of sagebrush assaulted my nostrils.

By the stars I knew we were traveling southwest. After
several hours we stopped, stripped the packs from our animals, and made ready to spend the night. A small stream
gurgled nearby. We made our bed of buffalo robes, and I lay
in Billy's arms. I silently thanked the Lord for him and
then drifted to sleep.

• CHAPTER SIXTEEN •

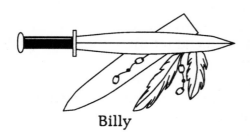

Billy

Like Lehi of old, Mae and I took our leave to flee into the wilderness. Under the cover of darkness we traveled, for we had enemies, and we didn't know who or how many. Folks had seen us spending Union Script at Fort Bridger and would be curious to know how much we had. But we had very little tucked away in my possibles bag, for money is a bother away from towns, and space is a premium.

After the first night, we traveled by day. Now and again Mae cast a glance to the north. My guess was that she was thinking of her mother. I thought of my own Shoshone family and the dreadful day in my eighth year when the Utes struck. We didn't have a chance. My father was killed, tomahawk in hand. He didn't go out alone. He took a whole passel of Ute warriors with him.

The Utes didn't scalp my father. It's an act of respect they give to an enemy warrior who has fought well. Nor did they violate my mother. They slit her throat, but she didn't struggle, 'cause she wasn't scared. She went into the World of Spirits with my father. I went into slavery . . . to the Ute village, led through the mountains with a thong tied around my neck.

I shook the thoughts of boyhood from my head and followed Mae's gaze to the north. By now Julienne and Hector would have joined an Oregon-bound wagon train.

I heard the report of the rifle and felt the jolt of the bullet at the same time. Someone screamed . . . surely it was Mae. I was falling, then a blanket of blackness spread over me.

When I woke it was night, and I was looking at the stars. For a moment I just lay there, trying to remember where I was and what had happened. I recalled that Mae and I had been riding southwest, and the Uinta Mountains were ahead. My head felt like it was on fire. Then I remembered the gunshot.

My headache was as big as a buffalo. Gingerly I put my fingers to my scalp and felt the clotted blood tracing the furrow of the bullet. I tried to rise to check for other wounds but was almighty dizzy and laid back down.

My gun belt and Smith and Wesson were missing. I put my hand to my knife. It was still there. The knife was double edged and razor sharp. I called it my Arkansas toothpick—it was a throwing knife. I kept it in a scabbard at the nape of my neck, between my shoulder blades. Whoever dry-gulched me either didn't care or hadn't thought to look for it. Nor did they remove the knife strapped to my leg.

They also left my bow on my back since bow and arrows are useless weapons for most white men. In my belt was a steel tomahawk, another useless weapon for most white men.

I thought of Mae . . . wondering . . . dreading. I must find her.

Again I tried to rise and this time I made it to my feet. But in a sudden wave of dizziness, I went down. The next time I opened my eyes the sun was hot above me. A cricket chirped and cicadas sang in the lazy afternoon. Not far away a stream gurgled. I looked at the hills, trying to determine if the stream was the Bear River, but I grew dizzy and my vision blurred.

My eyelids grew heavy so I closed them . . . but just for a minute. I opened them to complete darkness and shivered from the penetrating chill flowing down from the high Uintas, to the south.

I was drenched in sweat and shaking with chill. Looking at the millions of stars above, I started praying, pleading with the Lord for help, both for myself and for my bride.

The sound of the gurgling water reminded me that I desperately wanted a drink. Yet I was afraid I'd pass out again if I tried to stand. So on my hands and knees I crawled, inching my way through the willows to the stream. The cold water went down my throat like some crystalline elixir and gave me strength. Now I needed a fire.

Crawling back, I paused to gather and chew some of the inner bark of the willows. It's a medicine that eases pain, much like the inner bark of the aspen tree, except it isn't as effective.

In the sage, away from the creek, I collected fuel and struck a spark. I didn't build a large fire, but I used a small boulder for a reflector. The warmth felt good.

When the moon rose above the ridge I told my body to move, but my muscles did not respond. For just a minute I closed my eyes. When I opened them again my fire had burned down to the coals. Looking at the moon, I saw it had moved to the center of the heavens.

Again I willed my muscles to move. With great effort I stood on my two feet. Supporting myself with both hands on the boulder beside me, I counted the heavy throbs in my skull.

I rested my head against the boulder, closed my eyes and prayed. Then I made my way to the stream and again drank deeply of the cold water. In the willows I gathered a supply of the inner bark. Some I chewed, but most I tucked away in my medicine bag for future use. I moved back to my fire, added fuel, and slept the remainder of the night.

Come morning I felt better, though I could feel the throb of blood in my head. But it had been more than thirty-six hours since the dry-gulcher had cut me down and left me for dead. In the early morning light I studied the tracks and pieced together the story.

There were three attackers, riding horses with half worn shoes. I knew that the horse with the right hind hoof slightly turned in belonged to Harry. I wasn't surprised it was him. The horse with the wide horseshoes belonged to Mel. The third horse was a heavy horse, unfamiliar to me.

There was a trail from our camp made by eight horses—plain to see. It was wide enough that I could follow it at a run, which I thought I'd try as soon as my body was up to it. I started out walking, then I got brave and tried to run. I quickly got dizzy and fell. So I walked and I prayed. I prayed almighty hard for Mae. After a couple of hours my muscles limbered up and I seemed to grow in strength. By midmorning I was able to sustain a run.

Before noon I found where they had camped the night I'd been shot. Under a tree I found the spot where one of 'em had wrestled with Mae. It angered me to think of what they might have done to her. There were signs of a violent struggle.

What appeared to be a piece of meat, black with flies, caught my attention. I brushed away the flies and allowed myself a grin. It was the lobe of a human ear. Teeth marks indicated it had been bitten off. Yes siree, that Mae was a scrapper! I almost laughed, but then grew more somber. There was no way she could win in the end—less'n she got help.

Scouting for a trail, I found their tracks heading south, right into the Uintas. That surprised me because they didn't seem mountain wise. I'd have guessed they would have killed Mae, then struck a course for the Oregon Trail. But the tracks led south, so I followed.

The rider on the heavy horse rode beside Mae. Apparently he was her guard. Harry's horse flanked Mae on the outside. I got the idea they didn't trust each other, as there were signs that they were jockeying for position.

The tracks led higher into the mountains,. It skirted alpine lakes and crossed numerous streams. Then the trail veered to the southwest, more 'n likely to avoid the higher mountains. I found where they had shot some ducks and cleaned them before moving on.

My strength hadn't fully returned, but I was able to keep running now, gliding through the forest the way I'd been taught in my youth. It was the thought of Mae that kept me going.

Mid-afternoon I found where they had nooned the second day. We were traveling about the same speed . . . maybe I was a mite faster. It wasn't a very good place to noon as it bordered on some poison hemlock in full bloom. I also saw where the horses had cropped some brush. Looking at the brush I shook my head. They should have picketed their horses on the good grass by the lake, as that particular brush will give the horses gas . . . gas and a stomachache.

I found the discarded duck bones there. I cast around for signs, and saw where Mae had walked alone, more 'n likely to relieve herself. She had passed through a field of beautiful blue flowers. I looked in horror, as I saw where she had dug some of the bulbs.

They were death camas!

White camas are the edible camas. Their bulbs make an excellent addition for a duck stew. But blue camas is deathly poisonous.

Worried, I sat with my head in my hands and thought. What was going on? Was I going to lose Mae to poison? The Mormons say the Wasatch Mountains, to the east of the Salt Lake Valley, has more poisonous plants than any place on earth. If that's true, the Uinta Mountains are a close second. But Mae wouldn't know that, would she?

• CHAPTER SEVENTEEN •

Mae

This was not the way I'd planned on spending my honeymoon. Harry was in the lead, riding alone. Behind me was Mel, leading the string of horses. Beside me was a man called Bull. Bull was a paunchy man, but strong as an ox. It appeared that he had more brawn than brains. My hands were tied to the saddle horn. The cords cut my wrists.

With my own eyes I'd seen Billy killed. He'd fallen from his horse, dead, a bullet to the head. You never did see so much blood.

When the shot came, the pack horses started bucking. I'd just gotten 'em settled down and jumped to the ground to examine Billy, when Harry, Mel, and Bull rode up like charging buffaloes. I didn't have a chance.

Looking like he'd done something high and mighty, Harry set his horse while Mel and Bull jumped to the ground and tied my wrists. Then they sat me astride my horse and tied my hands to the saddle horn. Mel stripped Billy's Smith and Wesson from him, kicked him in the ribs, then spat on him. But you can't hurt a dead man.

"Please," I begged. "Kill me! I want to die with Billy!"

"There's time enough for that," Harry drawled, licking his lips as he thought. "First you'll be our woman."

I knew what he had in mind and it scared me. Yet, I

knew as long as I was alive there was a chance I could get even. They might put me through hell, but I would get them in the end. They weren't going to kill my man and just walk away . . . not by a darn sight!

"Fix us some grub, woman!" Harry ordered as we stopped for the night. He untied my hands, and we both knew escape was unlikely. But I was watching my chances all the same, keeping all my senses alert.

I started to unpack the cooking pots, moving slowly as these weren't men I wanted to please.

"If you decide to move too slow, I may have to hurry you up with a horse whip!" Harry said.

Bull stiffened, and I thought I saw something in his eye. He might appear big and dumb, but he acted mighty respectful around me. I had an idea he was like most western men in that he was respectful of all women. It was something to consider.

I fixed 'em supper, and a good supper it was. I had an idea now—an idea and a plan. It was rabbit stew that I fixed, and I ladled the choice portions to Bull. The gesture was not lost on Harry, who considered himself the cock of the roost. He eyed Bull several times and I knew there was going to be trouble. More 'n likely Bull knew it, too.

"I'll take the first watch," Harry said. "You're next, Bull, and you're last, Mel." He picked up his rifle, and slipped into the night.

I made my bed under a tree, and lay awake a long time. I was thinking of Billy . . . thinking and crying.

I guess I cried myself to sleep . . . I don't rightly know. I didn't sleep long before I suddenly woke to find Harry's weight a-top me. I smelled the awful stench of his breath as he tried to kiss me.

They say it takes up to four minutes to come all the way awake when you're deep in sleep, but I came out of my sleep like an angry squaw. I scratched and clawed, and I think Harry was enjoying it. Then I sunk my teeth into his ear with the intentions of chewing it right off . . . and I did, too. Yes sir, he screamed loud enough to wake the imps in hell. And when he pulled his head away, he left his ear lobe in my mouth.

I spat out his ear lobe and glared at him in the dark. He knocked me to the ground with a backhand to my face. Oh, that hurt, but being proud I sat back up. He backhanded me again, and I tried to get up again, but the world was spinning and I didn't know where the sky was. Grabbing me by the hair, Harry pulled me up only to knock me to the ground again. I was beyond crying; I was beyond terror. The only thought in my mind as I blacked out was that Harry was going to beat me to death before I had a chance to get even.

In my dreams demons were attacking me. They surrounded me and screamed in a horrifying way. I put my hands over my ears but the sound wouldn't go away. Then, in the midst of their screaming I heard another sound. It was the low, consistent, calming sound of an Indian chant. As it got louder the demons retreated. Finally their screaming stopped and the chant lifted me up into warm breezes that healed my body and soul. It wasn't until then that I recognized the voice doing the chanting.

"Billy," I cried.

When I opened my eyes it was broad daylight. I thought nightmares ended when you woke up, but mine hadn't. Harry was standing over me, horse whip in hand. His ear was bandaged. In his eyes was hatred . . . hatred like I'd never seen before. There was something else, too; there was insanity.

"You've done came to the end of your days," he said, and gave a sick chuckle like the demons in my dream. He raised his whip, and I knew it wouldn't rest until I was dead. But I didn't give him any satisfaction. I looked up into his eyes and said, "I told you yesterday to kill me, but you were too stupid to do it. I'm glad I maimed you!"

"Why you . . ."

What he was going to say didn't get said. It was the click of Bull's pistol being cocked that stopped him.

Both of us looked to Bull. No longer looking the part of the big dumb ox of the day before; he was a man sure of himself. And when Harry looked into the black hole of Bull's .45 he became an instant believer. But a man converted against his will is a convert in name only.

"There ain't going to be no woman-beating done in my presence, Boss. It just ain't proper!"

Oh, Harry didn't like it, he surely didn't! But he had enough savvy to know this wasn't the time to push Bull.

"Okay, Bull," he said. "Have it your way this time." Right then I knew Bull was as good as dead. Harry turned and never looked back. He went directly to the packs and started searching through 'em. Minutes later, he came stomping back.

"Where is it?" he demanded.

"Where is what?" I asked.

"Where is the money?"

"What money?"

"The money the Injun had! I know he had some, 'cause he spent some of it at Bridger!"

"He spent it all at Bridger," I replied. "Where do you think these supplies came from?"

"Mel," Harry accused. "You said the Injun had money!"

"He had it all right, Boss," Mel said. "I seen it big as life."

Harry looked at Bull, then back at Mel. "If he had money . . . I know where it is." Harry didn't press the issue any farther, but returned to the packs and started repacking. Both Bull and I knew what he was thinking. He was thinking that I'd given the money to Bull. Mel swore, knowing there was going to be trouble.

I was sick from the beating I'd taken but Harry wasn't feeling sorry for me. He demanded breakfast and I didn't dare deny him. I gingerly made my way to the fire and started slicing some salt bacon into a frying pan. The men ate hungrily, eating the bacon right out of the pan, leaving none for me. When the bacon was gone they sopped up the grease with some hard biscuits and wolfed them down.

Through it all, Harry and Bull both ate with their left hands, their right hands hovering close to their revolvers.

It was Mel that tied my hands to the saddle horn when we'd swung into the leather. As we moved out, I noted that both Harry and Bull held their reins with their left hand. We rode three abreast, with Bull to my right and Harry to my left. Behind us, Mel trailed with the string of horses.

Come noon I cooked some ducks Mel shot. The way they ate, you'd have thought I was the best cook in the west. Shucks, most any woman can cook if'n she has food to cook. My mother taught me the use of wild onions and herbs that grew wild in Texas. It makes all the difference, but you have to keep your eyes open for herbs.

In the West, many a man can tell you of trails they have never been on 'cause they learned to be good listeners. Us women are the same way; we can tell you of herbs and of different bulbs and roots that can be added to a stew even though we have never seen them before. So when I saw the death camas, I knew what they were, 'cause I'd heard Brother Campbell talk about 'em back at the Mormon wagon train. I decided they were my ace-in-the-hole. Yes sir, if'n something happened to Bull, I needed some way to get rid of Harry and Mel, and it had to be fast.

I don't know if Harry or Mel knew the difference between death camas and white camas, because their bulbs look alike. So I collected the bulbs and hid the flowers. Bringing back an apron of bulbs wasn't a thing to arouse suspicion.

We'd only been traveling a few hours after lunch when the horses started acting plumb miserable and some of 'em started passing gas. It was a sure sign that they'd munched on something that disagreed with them. Harry swore, but that was all that was said. The next lake they came to, they picketed the horses on the good grass along the shore, and Mel went fishing for our supper. He returned with a whole mess of fish.

We whiled away the afternoon, letting the horses get

over their colic. Bull and Harry eyed each other . . . brooding. Both knew a showdown was imminent.

I slept well that night but in the morning Bull and Harry didn't look like they had slept at all. The tension between them was so strong you could cut it with a knife. Clearly Harry avoided a direct conflict with Bull. My guess was he figured that in a direct conflict he might lose.

When the showdown finally came, it was quick and merciless, smacking of an assassination. It was mid-morning, and we were traveling through lodgepole pine. Suddenly a shot rang out, and Bull fell to the ground. Coolly, Harry thumbed a cartridge back into his pistol.

"He had it coming," Harry responded to Mel's questioning eyes. "Strip his gun belt and purse, and let's get going."

"You just a-goin' to leave him?"

"*You* want to bury him?" Harry threatened, his hand resting on the butt of his revolver.

"No," Mel hedged. "You're the boss." He swung down, and retrieved Bull's gun belt and possibles bag, then remounted.

What Harry figured to do with me, I could only guess. I'd lost my protector, and he'd be sorely missed. At least I had the camas bulbs. Tonight's supper would be special. My mind turned to Mama and Hector. If'n I got out of this, I'd join them.

• CHAPTER EIGHTEEN •

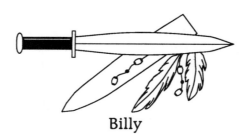

Billy

We Shoshone know how to run. When you're well you run 'cause it feels good. When you're sick you run 'cause it works like a sweat bath to drive out the evil spirits.

My dizziness ceased to be a major problem, and I was feeling good. The exuberance of the jog was in my blood. For hours I trotted a slow uphill trot. Harry and Mel had made no effort to hide their trail.

Suddenly I saw what appeared to be a downed animal directly ahead of me. I slowed my pace and put a hand on my tomahawk. The animal was lying atop the tracks I was following; it seemed out of place.

I saw as I drew closer that it was a human, not an animal. At first I thought it might be Mae, but discounted the idea, as Mae wasn't wearing buckskin.

Cautiously I looked around. The Uintas were dry, too dry for this time of year. The thin air was still and warm. The sky was bare of clouds. Where the sun reached the forest floor dry grass and dust gathered the heat. Earlier in the day I'd chewed on wild onions, and rubbed some on my skin as a hedge against insects.

Dust had settled on the body, indicating the man had lain there for some time. Still I took no chances and held my tomahawk in readiness.

A slight movement betrayed life. Depending on who he was, he might not be alive for long, though.

I snaked a knife from his belt. It was a heavy bowie knife, fifteen inches long with a hilt and cross-piece. I never had much use for a bowie knife myself, though many a knife fighter swears by 'em. I extracted a second knife from his boot—a thin Spanish stiletto made of fine steel.

The man had been shot in the back, through his left chest. The bullet had come dangerously close to his heart and spine. Froth came from the bullet hole when I turned him over.

He looked up into my eyes. It was a pleading look, but I didn't offer to help him 'til I'd bound his hands. I'm just not a trusting soul, though I did bind his hands in front of him. Cutting material from his buckskin shirt, I forced a piece of leather into the bullet holes, front and back, to keep his lung from collapsing.

"It's up to you to live or die," I announced when finished. It was the first words I had spoken. "If you want to live, you can breathe easier if you lie on your wounded side. But you've got to force both of your lungs to work, even if you spit blood. If you don't, you'll die of consumption."

He looked grateful, but then I threw the fear of God in him. I took out my razor sharp knife, showed him how sharp it was, then announced, "I'm Shoshone. My people are experts at skinning prisoners alive. Start telling me about my wife."

"I ain't got nothing to hide, Injun," he said, looking ominously at my skinning knife. "She's okay . . . at least she was when I saw her last. I sided with her. Kept Harry from whipping her, I did."

"You were one of 'em who shot me!" I accused.

"Harry is the one who shot you. He said you had money, a lot of it. He shot *me* 'cause I was trying to protect your woman."

"Harry shot you?"

"Yes."

"That figures. He isn't too sharp at his shooting."

"He got lead into both of us," the big man said testily.

"True," I said, with a grin. "But getting lead into a body

and killing him are two different things. Even a pilgrim knows that." I thought I saw him smile. "So, you got a name?"

"They call me Bull, and it's as good a name as any. I stuck up for your woman. I've done many a lowdown thing in my life, but I ain't no woman killer." It figured.

"That woman o' yours, she's got spunk . . . bit Harry's earlobe right off. He's got a fierce temper and was beating her senseless, 'til I pulled him off. I just don't hold to woman beating."

I liked Bull, though he surely was running with bad company. "I'll move you beside the stream," I said, releasing the cords that bound him. "But I can't stay with you 'cause I have to find my woman before Harry kills her."

"Off hand," Bull noted, "I'd say that woman of yours will take a lot. I think Harry is in more danger than he thinks."

I hoped he was right.

I moved Bull to a secluded spot near a stream and spent the night. He was shaking with chills. He'd likely survive if he fought it, but he'd die if he gave in. I had an idea he was a fighter.

As the sun's rays grew in the east we breakfasted on nettle and ground squirrel. Then, leaving Bull to fight for his life, I started off at a trot following Mel, Harry, and Mae.

Mid-morning I smelled smoke. Wary, I drifted like a shadow from shade to shade, stalking the source of the smell as a man stalks an animal. Carefully I zeroed in and sneaked up on the camp. Harry was standing, but looking almighty sick. Another person who I took for Mel was still in his sleeping roll. "Where is she?" I demanded as I stepped into the clearing. With an arrow fit to my bowstring, I was ready. Startled, he looked at me. He was a sick man.

"She poisoned us and lit out," he said. He was judging me, calculating his chances. His chances of getting away from me were slim, and he knew it. With nothing to lose, he suddenly went for his gun, and I let my arrow fly. It flew true and buried itself in Harry's chest.

A deer can run fifty or more yards after being shot in the heart, and men are not all that different. After I'd shot Harry, he started repeatedly pulling the trigger of my Smith and Wesson .44, which he'd laid claim to. I dove for the cover of a nearby tree. The bullets missed me, but they didn't miss Mel, who was rolled in his blankets between Harry and me.

Face down, Harry hit the dirt. His body gave a few jerks as the reports from his pistol rolled off the hills, and then it was over.

I read the signs and figured Mae lit out during the night. Apparently she'd fed Harry and Mel some death camas, then made good her escape. Whether they would have died from the camas I'll never know.

I buried them there, on a beautiful slope in the Uintas. Their graves weren't deep, 'cause if you have ever been in the Uinta's, you know that the Great Spirit created the range of mountains out of rocks and then sprinkled a little soil over the top of them. As time was critical I wanted to leave them for the prowling carnivores, but Mae and her family had convinced me that civilized people bury the dead. So I did.

My aching heart told me to follow my bride as quickly as possible and resume our honeymoon. But back along the trail I'd left a man with my enemy's bullet in his chest fighting for his life. Bull would need his weapons if a pack of wolves should come upon him. And he'd need his gear and mount. He'd come to the aid of my woman when she needed him, so I mounted up, gave one longing look at Mae's trail, and struck a course back to Bull.

• Chapter Nineteen •

Mae

It was duck stew I made for Harry and Mel. I started cooking as soon as Harry declared camping time. I was scared, 'cause I knew Harry wouldn't put up with me for long. Before he had a chance to get ideas for the evening, I filled the forest with the sweet smells of cooking that made the men's mouths water.

After I'd put stew on, using liberal amounts of onions and herbs from the forest, I started a batch of biscuits. Often I tasted the stew, making sure they saw me. Then, with the stew halfway done, I added the camas. I waited a few minutes, then plopped the biscuits into the hot Dutch oven, making it a perfectly timed meal.

Selfish men, they ate like animals, as if there was no tomorrow. I knew that if I didn't fend for myself, there would be no food left. I made a show of grabbing for a biscuit to avoid suspicion.

After they had finished there was nothing left of the meal. A lone wild duck isn't much for two selfish men. I had to think of something to keep them occupied while they digested their camas so I started whipping up a batch of dough.

"What ya making," Harry demanded.

"Bear signs," I replied, hoping he'd allow me to continue. I didn't have much to worry about, as men with a diet of mostly meat crave pastry. Harry sat on his haunches, chewing a wad of pine gum, biding his time. He intended to have his fun with me eventually, I was sure.

It takes time to cook a batch of bear signs, and I made a large batch. We had camped long before dark, but when dusk came, I was still cooking the bear signs. By then Harry and Mel appeared to have something on their mind besides pastry; they weren't feeling so good.

Suddenly Harry got an unholy look in his eyes and I figured he decided that he'd been served tainted food. He went to his pack, where he kept a horsewhip, but in the brief moment his back was turned, I lit out.

"Come back, you heathen witch," he screamed, and accented his point by cracking his whip. But my mom didn't raise no dummies. I was high-tailing it through timber like a jack rabbit not giving him a good shot at me if'n he took a notion to use his gun. I figured I could outrun him. I figured correctly.

I hung around in the darkness outside of camp for a long time, 'cause I wanted my horse. Both Harry and Mel were freely groaning and cursing. They were sick. In addition to my horse I wanted Billy's Appaloosa and a little grub too.

As their cursing lost its vigor, I slipped off my shoes and crept to the horses. Carefully I felt for twigs with my bare feet. Placing my weight first on the outside of my foot, then rolling it in, the way Billy taught me, I slid silently through the forest.

The horse I'd been riding was a strawberry roan with three white stockings. He had been a mustang but had good blood in him. The roan made no fuss as I led him to the saddles. Then I repeated the process with Billy's mare.

My first objective achieved, I decided to try for my bedroll and a sack of grub, which rested near the dying fire. An owl hooted a warning, but I paid it no mind. I creeped along slowly, taking my time.

My hand on my bedroll I tucked it under my left arm and reached for a sack of grub in my right. Mel stirred, and I froze for an instant. When he became still, I backed into the darkness.

The operation successful, I tied the bedroll and grub securely to Billy's saddle. But confident with my success, I became greedy and eyed Mel's rifle leaning against a tree. Slowly I inched my way to the tree, being careful not to look directly at Mel or Harry, 'cause Billy says you can sometimes feel the eyes of an enemy watching you. But it was I who felt the enemy's eyes.

Suddenly I glanced at Harry and saw his hot, hard eyes following me. He was lifting his pistol, but was having a hard time mastering the heavy weapon.

I dove for the rifle. Out of the corner of my eye I noted that Harry was having trouble focusing his eyes. Rifle in hand I grabbed the sack of bear signs and scampered through the forest like a scared deer.

I tried to slide the rifle into Billy's rifle scabbard. To my surprise the scabbard already contained a rifle, *Billy's* rifle. I'd risked getting the rifle for nothing, yet I had the bear signs, which would taste almighty good in a few hours. So I slid the rifle into my bedroll and swung into the leather. The way Harry looked, he wouldn't be pursuing anyone for a while, but come daylight I intended to be a long way from there.

Keeping the big drinking gourd of the starry sky to my right, I rode into the night. Somewhere ahead was the valley of the Great Salt Lake. I didn't know how far. When I got out of the mountain, I'd bear to the right and see if I could pick up the Mormon Trail.

I became acutely aware of the sounds of the night. Crickets chirped, and an owl hooted. The stately lodge pole pines gave way to grotesque juniper trees. Because I trusted his eyesight more than my own, I let my horse pick his way and choose his own speed. We were making poor time.

Thinking of my man, I rode. For many days I'd been brave, but suddenly my pent up emotions got the best of me, and I cried. I just rode along, crying in the darkness and not caring.

When the sun rose behind me in the east, ahead lay a long valley. Snaking its way through the valley, a lazy stream flowed. I rode down to the stream where the grass was green and lush. I picketed my horses and curled up in the morning sun to sleep. Once, I woke and saw that the sun was two hands high in the eastern sky, but I turned over and went back to sleep.

Suddenly I was awakened. Something was wrong! I lay still, trying to awaken completely before I moved. I became aware of the breeze in the pine boughs.

Then it came again, a slight nudge. I peeked out of one eye and then grinned. It was Billy's Appaloosa nudging me.

"Do you think it's time to go?" I asked, talking to the old mare as Billy would. The mare snorted . . . sometimes she was almost human.

Saddling up, I followed the stream at an easy walk. The stream led west, then turned north. I figured that eventually it would empty into the Great Salt Lake. But to the west was high, snowcapped mountains, so I wondered.

Late afternoon I crossed what I took for the Mormon Trail. It was time for me to decide if I was going to turn west to Salt Lake or east to Fort Bridger and the Oregon Trail. Since this was as good a place as any to camp, I settled down for the night.

• CHAPTER TWENTY •

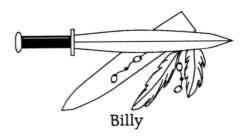

Billy

Though anxious to follow Mae's trail, I felt duty bound
to retrace my own steps to where I'd left Bull. "Hello the
fire," I called as I drew near. Though I knew Bull didn't
have a gun, proper etiquette is always in order.

"That you, Billy?" came a weak reply.

"It's me," I said as I walked up to my former enemy. He
didn't look good. "I see you're too ornery to die."

"Ain't feeling ornery right now," he responded, "I feel
meek as a lamb."

"Meekness is good for the soul, they say."

"What does an Indian know about the soul?" he retorted,
a twinkle in his hot eyes.

"I'm a Christian Indian."

"You weren't very Christian when you threatened to skin
me alive."

"You weren't very Christian when you helped set me up
for killing," I replied. "Besides, I come bearing gifts, like the
three wise man." He looked at the string of horses I trailed,
and his eyes brightened.

"Mighty thoughtful. I don't suppose Harry had a turn of
heart and decided to return 'em without being persuaded."

"I helped him to see the error of his ways, though I don't
know as he is a believer yet. And Mel got in the way of
Harry's bullets; all his meanness oozed out."

"Where's Mae?"

"She made her escape last night. Seems she cooked a duck stew which contained death camas. It took the steam right out o' her captors' sails. More 'n likely it would have killed 'em if'n they hadn't died a more violent death."

Bull grinned. "Harry just didn't give womenfolk enough credit, especially that woman of yours. The minute he laid hold of her, he was in trouble."

With his skin so pale, Bull looked like death-warmed-over. But he seemed feisty, determined to fight for his life.

"We better get you setting upright, then get you used to walking, before you climb into the saddle," I suggested.

He grunted, and I helped him to his feet. After a few minutes he eased himself into his saddle and we moved out. He rode upright like a man should ride, yet I tied his hands to the saddle horn lest he pass out and fall.

We went south to where I'd buried Harry and Mel. Then we followed Mae's trail west. It wasn't hard to follow 'cause she hadn't made any effort to hide it.

It was a slow go of it, but Bull was game. Still, I had to make time before the rains came. August days in the Uintas are hot and the nights cold 'cause the thin air doesn't hold much heat. But most every afternoon it clouds up and rains on the western slopes, which would wipe out Mae's tracks. Still, this was a dry year; maybe the rains wouldn't come.

Squirrels chattered and a golden eagle dove to the earth, snatching prey in its claws. A porcupine ambled across a log, content with itself and the world.

You never saw so many deadfalls . . . deadfalls and rocks. But apparently Mae had given my Appaloosa her head, and the mare had followed game trails. Still, Bull was a big man, riding a horse 'bout seventeen hands high, so he had to duck under many a tree. The trees were mostly lodge pole pine. Lodge pole pine grow straight and tall and lose their needles down low. But they retain a lot of scratchy twigs that can wipe a man right off a horse.

We passed from the pines to the junipers, following
Mae's trail to the foothills. By a meandering beaver stream,
we found pressed down grass—evidence that she'd slept
there for a long time, maybe all morning. We weren't making very good time, but she hadn't made good time either.

"You hanging in there?" I asked Bull. He said nothing. I
looked back at him and saw him bent forward over his saddle, unconscious. Nudging my horse next to him, I lifted his
head to examine him. Out of the corner of my eye, I saw
movement. It was a rabbit breaking for its hole. I pawned my
.44 and felt it buck. The rabbit wasn't nearly fast enough.

Easing Bull to the ground, I laid him on a blanket, and
noticed him looking into my eyes, his hot face pained. "Am I
still alive?" he asked, forcing a grin.

"I have to keep watching you now and again to make
sure, but I think you're too mean to die."

"That was good shooting."

"I thought you were passed out."

"Maybe I was before you lifted my head, I don't know.
But as you say, I'm too mean to die."

I handed him some mountain yarrow and inner aspen
bark I'd picked up along the way. "You chew this," I ordered,
"and I'll have food ready directly." He turned up his nose, as
mountain yarrow is almighty bitter. But he took it and
chewed, knowing it was good for his fever.

The afternoon showers came as we were eating our
meal, but didn't last long. The rain effectively wiped out
Mae's trail, but we were out of the mountain now, and had
a good idea where she was headed.

The shower over, Bull saw me looking to the north. "I
can stand to ride another few miles," he said.

"I don't know . . .," I said, eyeing him.

"We both know the Mormon Trail hain't far away, and
we hain't many hours behind Mae.

He was right and we both knew it. So we remounted and
followed the creek north.

Into the night we rode. Only when it was full dark did
we stop. I was sure we were near the Mormon Trail. I eased

Bull to the ground and made him as comfortable as possible under a juniper. Checking the load in his pistol, I placed it near him, along with a canteen.

"When I return don't shoot me," I grinned. "I'll announce my coming with the yip of a fox."

"How am I to tell you from the real thing?" he questioned. "You Indians are so darn good at it, I can't even hear the echo."

"Good point, Bull. Let's change it to the hoot of an owl, 'cause you're not likely to be shooting at an owl. Can you answer back?"

"Yeah."

"Let me hear you." He hooted weakly.

"Well," I grinned. "There's not much chance of me mistaking that hoot for the real owl." Despite himself, he managed a smile.

I slipped into the night, keeping an eye out for the outline of horses. Now and again I tested the air with my nose for horse. Their smell is distinct. I'd also imitate a whinny now and again 'cause horses are social creatures and will answer a whinny. But it was the horses that found me. As good as my sense of smell is, horses' sense of smell is better.

The low whinny of my Appaloosa brought me up short. I'd raised her from a colt . . . raised her on love and carrots, and I'd owned her mother before her. She was both an Indian pony and a white man's horse; I could mount her from the right like an Indian or from the left like a white man.

Following the whinny, I carefully eased along. Mae might be jumpy and quick to shoot, thinking I was an enemy.

I saw the red coals of her fire first. Behind it, back to a boulder, she was curled up in a bedroll, using the boulder for a reflector. Unless I missed my guess, she would be sleeping with a pistol in her hand.

I gave the call of a quail that I'd taught her out on the prairie. She didn't respond and I grew worried.

Inch by inch I moved to her buffalo robe bedroll. Her head was under the covers, but when I was almost atop her

I could see her locks of brown hair. I could see something
else, too—the tip of a revolver poking out from under the
covers.

Carefully I put my hand on the weapon and slid it from
her grasp.

Suddenly she awakened and broke the stillness of the
night with a gosh-awful scream. She flung the corner of the
buffalo robe aside, and I caught the flicker of a knife in the
starlight. Her well aimed thrust came so close it cut my
buckskin shirt.

"Mae! It's me, Billy!" I screamed as I jumped back.
Though Mae could be soft as a kitten, I was fast learning
that she fought like a mountain lion. She hesitated, peering
into the darkness.

"B . . . Billy?

"It's me, Mae."

"Can't be. I saw them kill you . . . kick you . . . spit on
you."

"I ain't dead, Mae, at least not so you'd notice."

She threw off the buffalo robes faster 'un scat and
jumped into my arms. I held her for a few minutes feeling
the tremble of her body—feeling the tremble of my own.
Then she started crying, but she was okay. She pulled me
down to the buffalo robes and we lay in each other's arms,
happy to still be in this world together. Gradually the
weariness of the last few days drained from us, and we
slept. We'd been hard used, but had come through.

• CHAPTER TWENTY-ONE •

Mae

It was gray in the east, Billy slipped out of our bedroll. I knew where he was going . . . to the creek for his early morning bath, followed by his private morning devotional.

For a while I waited, then I made up my mind. I slipped out from under the buffalo robes and slipped on my moccasins. Quietly I followed him.

As Billy stood there, watching the sun peek over the eastern hills, I quietly slid in beside him. Together we observed the Great Silence.

Prayer over, he looked me full in the face. I grinned, shrugged my shoulders and said, "I guess you're stuck with me, Billy."

He took me in his arms and gave an amused chuckle. "I guess we've started our first family tradition. Though, it's not new, 'cause Mormon's teach couples that they should pray both silently and together."

The spot where Bull had spent the night was less than a mile away. With the new rays of sunlight fresh in the east, Billy and I walked hand in hand to Bull's camp.

White and stiff, Bull looked more dead than alive. Still he was sitting up, and managed a grin as we walked up.

"See you found your woman," he observed. "Harry would have done well to have left her alone."

"He would have, at that. It never pays to take a woman too lightly."

"How ya feeling this morning?" I put in.

"I think I'm on the mend," he said as boldly as he could, but grimacing with pain.

"You hungry?"

"No."

"Not even for bear signs?"

His eyes brightened up. "Now that's a different story."

"We came to move you down to our camp on the Mormon Trail. When we get there we'll let you have-at the bear signs."

"Let's get going," he replied weakly, but with a little more enthusiasm.

"I'll fetch your mount," Billy replied as he hefted Bull's saddle.

"You can fetch my mount, Billy, but as for ridin', I think I'd rather walk. It'll do me good."

The walk to our camp about did Bull in. But he was game and didn't complain. I knew he wouldn't.

Watching the northeast horizon as we munched our bear signs, we observed an ever increasing cloud of dust.

"That dust plume—how far away would you say it is?" Billy asked.

"Don't know," I replied. "You're better at judging distance than I."

"If it's a wagon company, I'd say they're likely a day's travel away, 'bout fifteen miles."

"Sounds about right."

"We could ride out and meet 'em, and leave Bull here to rest, or we can rest up today and wait for 'em to come to us.

"Let's wait," I said. Then added, "Do you think it is the Flake Company?"

"Could be, but I think Flake Company should be in Salt Lake by now. Still, there wasn't a company very close behind them."

We rested, bathed in the cold stream, washed our clothes, and prepared to meet the company. Come evening, we looked the part of a honeymooning couple. Bull too, seemed to perk up. His fever seemed to be breaking.

With the late afternoon sun at our backs, Billy and I set our mounts as the company came into view. Bull was back in camp leaning against a tree.

In the clouds of dust it was hard to see, but the lead rider rode tall in the saddle, like Brother Flake. I caught my breath, hoping it was him.

"It *is* him!" I squealed, as they grew closer. Billy grinned and we booted our mounts into a gallop.

Brother Flake broke into a broad smile as we rode up and bucked our horses to a halt on either side of him. "It surely took you long enough to get here," Billy said.

"Some of the oxen came down with the colic," he explained. "Oxen with the colic are worse than children, you know." We knew.

"You two look mighty fresh for a honeymooning couple. What have you been doing with yourself?"

"Honeymooning is hard work, Brother Flake. But we had the day to rest up while you moseyed along."

Flake eyed the scab that furrowed Billy hair. "Looks like you got a new part in your hair."

"It was nothing," Billy lied. "Just Mae shaping me up."

"Billy Harold!" I teased. "You quit lying that way!" Brother Flake chuckled, but by then the lead wagon had stopped, and a small crowd had collected.

"Corral!" Flake shouted. Then he said, "I was going to camp here anyway."

We dismounted, and were hard pressed with everyone talking at once. Ellen was at my elbow trying to tell me something about my mother. Suddenly Hector pushed his way through the crowd and hurled himself into my arms. He hugged me tight and said, "I knew you'd come back. Now Billy will have time to teach me to be an Indian—a Shoshone Indian."

There were a hundred questions I wanted to ask, but this was not the time for words. Then someone threw her arms around both of us, and I looked into Mama's wet eyes.

"Weren't you going to Oregon?" I questioned, after we'd hugged.

"After you left, Oregon didn't seem so important. So when Brother Flake argued that I ought to winter with the Mormons, I gave in."

"Are you going on to Oregon in the spring?"

"I can't rightly say," she replied. "Even the prospect of gold doesn't seem as important this year as last."

That night we all sat around the fire swapping stories. There was Mama and Hector and Ellen and Brother Flake and many others. At first Billy and I had been sitting beside each other; but when he got up to get a drink of water his place beside me was taken by Marion Camp, one of the girls I met when we first joined the Mormon wagon train. Billy found a spot directly opposite the fire from me. There was laughter and singing and happy voices; but as I looked across the top of the fire into Billy's eyes, those sounds faded and in their place I again heard a chant—a Shoshone chant. Billy heard it, too. It seemed to be coming down from the stars and up from the earth at the same time. It was as if all creation were singing. I don't know Shoshone, but the chant filled me with joy. I think it wouldn't be too far off to say the chant was about how right it was for white and Indian to be sitting together in peace—but then it could hae been about just how right it was to be in love.

More Great Books

from

Dating, No Guts, No Glory, a novel *by Joni Hilton.* In this sequel to *Braces, Gym Suits, and Early Morning Seminary,* we maneuver with Louisa Barker through the thrills and spills of Datingdom.

Soft Cover $6.95

Where Eagles Rest, *by Hyrum Smith,* helps youth to see more clearly, set higher goals, and be motivated to positive actions. From Vietnam to Hawaii to his own home, he draws powerful analogies and lessons for life that will linger in your mind

Soft Cover $5.95

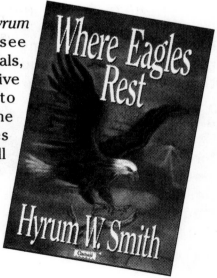

Tennis Shoes Among the Nephites, *by Chris Heimerdinger,* is a spellbinding novel that takes you back in time for a modern adventure in an ancient Book of Mormon land. It brings Book of Mormon characters to life! This novel is carefully researched so that the reader learns hundreds of things about the Book of Mormon. So intriguing for all ages that it is one of your best gift choices.

Soft Cover $7.95

Gadiantons and the Silver Sword, *by Chris Heimerdinger.* In Heimerdinger's latest, the characters from *Tennis Shoes Among the Nephites* are reunited in an explosive saga that transports you from Utah and the American West to southern Mexico and its deep, shadowy jungles. Experience the adventure as Jim Hawkins, his sister, Jennifer, and Garth Plimpton stay one step ahead of the Gadiantons in a quest that teaches them the true meaning of valiance.

Soft Cover $7.95